WITHDRAWN

Studies in German Literature, Linguistics, and Culture:
Literary Criticism in Perspective

Ludwig Emil Grimm's illustration for "Hänsel und Gretel" from
Kinder- und Hausmärchen gesammelt durch die Brüder Grimm,
32nd ed. (Cotta, 1906)

James M. McGlathery

Grimms' Fairy Tales

A History of Criticism on a Popular Classic

C AMDEN H OUSE

Published by Camden House, Inc.
Drawer 2025
Columbia, SC 29202 USA

Printed on acid-free paper.
Binding materials are chosen for strength and
durability.

ISBN:1-879751-90-9

LIBRARY OF CONGRESS CATALOGING-IN-PUBLICATION DATA

McGlathery, James M., 1936-
    Grimms' fairy tales : a history of criticism on a popular classic
/ James M. McGlathery
    p. cm. -- (Studies in German literature, linguistics, and culture.
Literary criticism in perspective)
        Includes bibliographical references and index.
        ISBN 1-879751-90-9 (acid-free paper)
        1. Kinder- und Hausmärchen. 2. Grimm, Jacob, 1785-1863--Criticism
and interpretation. 3. Grimm, Wilhelm, 1786-1859--Criticism and interpretation.
4. Fairy tales--Germany--History and criticism. 5. Folklore--Germany. I. Title
II. Series.
PT921.M38   1993
398.21'0943--dc20   93-37093
                                                                        CIP

Contents

In Memoriam

Ernst Alfred Philippson   1900-1992

Preface

FAIRY TALES BELONG TO popular culture, yet some of them equally well among the great literary classics. Few people the world over have no notion of what fairy tales are or have had no contact with them. Most people, at the same time, would not imagine that fairy tales have been the subject of much scholarly debate, literary criticism, and interpretive speculation. To the popular mind, and indeed to most educated general readers, fairy tales simply are as they seem and require no commentary or analysis. It is not always clearly understood that fairy tales, in the forms we know them, are products of sophisticated literary creators or transmitters. The type of story that most of us would immediately recognize and accept as a proper fairy tale is no older, really, than those by Charles Perrault, told to suit sophisticated French literary tastes at the end of the seventeenth century, during the reign of Louis XIV. Our English term 'fairy tale' is a translation of the French *conte de fées*, which came into currency only in Perrault's day. We are, at the same time, dimly aware that fairy tales, as we know and cherish them, are indeed literary creations, for we associate them most readily with the names of Hans Christian Andersen, the Danish author; the German Grimm brothers; and, to a lesser extent, Perrault. Still, the general perception is that such tales, if products of the literary imagination, are simple narratives in no need of critical or scholarly study.

Generally speaking, fairy tales are not perceived, either, to belong so very specially to folklore and folktale. When one thinks of this type of traditional oral narrative there come first to mind ghost stories, legends, tall tales, jokes, anecdotes, and all other manner of funny or terrifying stories, as well as narratives with religious import of one type or another, such as myths and pious tales. Fairy tale tends to be viewed as somewhat apart from folktale, not least because fairy tales as we know them came to be shaped in particular literary ways. Furthermore, in this century most people's familiarity with fairy tales has occurred through what we have come to call the commercial media, indeed through comic books, radio, and television. This development has particular meaning for me, since it dates from my early childhood in the 1930s and 1940s, and extended through my experiences of parenthood in the 1960s and 1970s. My birth roughly coincided with the release of Walt Disney's *Snow White and the Seven Dwarfs* and the beginnings of the craze for comic books; and aside from the Disney films, my acquaintance with fairy tales was almost wholly from the Saturday morning radio program *Let's Pretend*, to which I listened avidly as a child in the 1940s.

Scholarly interest in fairy tale, however, arose precisely because of perceived ties between those stories and myth and legend. Beginning with Jacob and Wilhelm Grimm themselves, fairy tales began to be studied as descending from ancient sources, and therefore as providing information about the past of nations and peoples and as preserving remnants of cultural treasures otherwise lost or unrecorded. As a consequence, study of fairy tale in the Grimms' time and on to the end of the nineteenth century was almost wholly devoted either to attempts at determining the place and time of the genre's origin or at discovering in the tales survivals of ancient ritualistic practices.

Only around the beginning of the twentieth century did the study of fairy tale as a literary genre begin in earnest. At the same time, ideologies arising with the new century sought to discover meanings in the tales which accorded with their philosophy. Literary scholarship in this century has been predominantly concerned with distinguishing fairy tale from other genres in popular narrative. Here again, the Grimms' collection has been at the forefront; for it has been their tales, together with those of Perrault, which have provided the model for investigation, so that some scholars came to speak of a 'Grimmian genre' or 'tales à la Grimm.' Similarly, much of the other literary scholarship has been concerned with Wilhelm Grimm's stylization of the tales as found in his sources, and changes he made during the course of reworking or adapting the stories, while similar stylistic studies have been made of the collections by Perrault and his Neapolitan predecessor Giambattista Basile (his *Pentamerone* of the earlier seventeenth century). The question of the meaning of fairy tales was largely left to the ideological critics: anthroposophists, nationalists, existentialists, Marxists, and others, but most especially critics oriented toward one variety or another of psychoanalytic theory.

Among folklorists, there was a gradual shift away from the geographical-historical approach, concerned with the distribution, transmission, and origins of tales, as fostered by the so-called Finnish school through its Folklore Fellows Communications, dating from the twentieth century's first decade. Folklorists in the second half of the century have devoted their attention rather to the relation between particular versions of stories and the cultures—and levels of society—in which the versions are found, as well as to storytelling as a performing art that tailors itself to specific audiences. Thus, like literary scholars, folklorists came to focus more on the artistic qualities of fairy tale; and like ideologically oriented critics, they became more inclined to address the question of interpretation, albeit most often with regard to cultural as opposed to theoretical contexts.

The present study attempts to provide an account of criticism on fairy tale as it pertains to the Grimms' *Children's and Household Tales* (their *Kinder- und Hausmärchen*, 1812, 1815). It is perhaps regrettable that this account cannot be given in the form of a linear narrative after the manner of the fairy tales themselves. The story is too complex for that. What I have done instead is begin with a chapter on folktale scholarship generally, then follow it with a chapter about study and criticism on the Grimms' collection specifically, and conclude with a chapter on commentary about the individual tales. Some attempt has been made within each chapter to give a chronological account, but even here it has seemed better to do so with regard to particular subjects or categories of scholarship, rather than for the entire matter. I have tried, though, to convey a sense of when each type of criticism first arose and to place its beginnings in chronological relationship to the start of other types of commentary. Likewise, wherever I have found it possible, I have attempted to locate the origins of particular critical directions in the intellectual, cultural, and political history of the times, in accord with the aim of the series *Literary Criticism in Perspective*, of which this volume is a part.

The account given here is of course not the whole story. I have excluded journalistic commentary on folktale and fairy tale as well as the entire matter of the reception of the Grimms' tales as reflected, too, in parodies, adaptations, and other creative reactions and responses. The scope has been limited to what may be termed scholarly studies, together with interpretive criticism based in ideological theory. Even within this limitation, the survey is not complete. My aim has been rather to include sufficient breadth and depth to give a good accounting and representative picture of the various types of scholarship and commentary and an outline of their development. Finally, the purpose of an account such as this militates against fuller exposition of given critical positions. Instead, the aim has been to fit the work of particular individuals into the context of the whole without misrepresenting them.

Because *Grimms' Fairy Tales* is a popular classic, I have tried to render this account intelligible to general readers who have no specialized background in literary or folkloristic studies. I would count among such readers American undergraduate students, to whom I wish to address myself particularly. For graduate students in literature or folklore, too, I believe that there is sufficient detail for profitable reading. And I hope that even specialists in the study of fairy tales and folktales will find here matters of which they may have been unaware, or which they will see in new contexts.

4

Citation of all sources is given in parentheses in the text, e.g. (Rölleke, 1986a, 101-02). In this example, the reference is to an essay by the foremost contemporary authority on *Grimms' Fairy Tales*, Heinz Rölleke, published in 1986, with the full bibliographical information given under that year in the chronologically arranged bibliography at the end of the volume (for each year, the entries are given in alphabetical order by the last name of the author or editor). The 'a' after 1986 in the example indicates that the reference is the first of the three items cited for Rölleke for that year. The page numbers following "1986a" refer to the publication actually cited or quoted, in this case a 1988 English translation of the original 1986 essay in German, as indicated in the bibliographical information provided for this entry. All quotations are given in English, and except where otherwise indicated, the translations from German and other languages are my own. At the head of the bibliography there is a selective list of editions of the Grimms' tales, as well as shorter lists for the collections of Perrault and Basile.

Much of the research for the present volume was done while I was writing my interpretive study of the Grimms' tales, *Fairy Tale Romance* (1991), which dealt with the stories about love and marriage and compared them with those in the earlier literary collections by Basile and Perrault. Neither that project nor the additional work done for this account of criticism on the Grimms' collection could have been completed without the help of the interlibrary loan service of the University of Illinois. For each of the two projects, the Research Board of this campus's Graduate College provided grants for assistants, whose help has been greatly appreciated: Ann Michels for the earlier work and Evelyn Abdallah for the present study.

1: The Folktales

THE GRIMM BROTHERS' COLLECTION of folktales, their *Kinder- und Hausmärchen* (1812, 1815), is of course famous the world over. Less well known is that Jacob and Wilhelm Grimm may also be credited with founding the study of folktale as a scholarly field. The Grimms, indeed, were not the first to publish a collection of stories purportedly told by common people. The early seventeenth-century Neapolitan author Giambattista Basile's posthumously published *Pentamerone* (originally titled *Lo cunto de li cunti*, 1634-36) portrayed the tellers of the fifty stories there as being ten of the ugliest old women and best storytellers around. That claim, though, was not necessarily to be taken seriously, for it is made within the frame story and is itself thus part of the fiction; and Basile certainly did not provide any information whatsoever about his sources for the stories. Similarly, the French courtier, royal official, and author Charles Perrault, in his *Tales of Mother Goose* (*Contes de ma mère l'Oye*, 1695) and his *Histoires ou contes de temps passé* (1697), claimed to have his tales from the folk yet, like Basile, did not say how or exactly from whom. Not until the Grimms, with their notes to the two volumes of their first edition of the *Kinder- und Hausmärchen* (1812; 1815) was information given about sources, beyond the vague claim—not always seriously meant—that the tales were from the folk.

The Grimms' annotations—expanded for the second edition (1819) in which they were accorded a volume of their own (1822)—added a scholarly dimension to what had hitherto been a purely literary enthusiasm. The Grimms' indication, however vague, of the region from which they had a particular story, or version of a story, encouraged others to try their hand at collecting tales from storytellers and to compare the stories with those in the Grimms' collection. The Grimms, indeed, encouraged others in this endeavor and even published an invitation to submit such material to them. Of particular importance for the early history of folktale study, though, was the assumption—like that of the English scholar Thomas Percy (*Reliques of Ancient Poetry*, 1765), Goethe's contemporary Johann Gottfried Herder (*Volkslieder*, 1778/1779), and the Grimms' own literary friends Achim von Arnim and Clemens Brentano (*Des Knaben Wunderhorn: Alte Deutsche Lieder*, 1806, 1808; The Boys' Horn of

Plenty: Old German Songs) for folksong—that these stories preserved material from earlier, even prehistoric times. The result was that folktales came to be studied first with regard to the question of their origins.

As members of the Romantic generation in Germany—those authors, artists, and scholars born mostly in the 1770s and 1780s who therefore entered adulthood in the period of the French Revolution and Napoleon's ensuing conquests—the Grimms were particularly interested in recovering and rediscovering the Germanic past in particular. Their famous dictionary of the German language and most of their other scholarly writing and editing was motivated by that enthusiasm and concern. Similarly, although they were acutely aware that the folktales in their collection, by and large, belonged to shared European traditions of storytelling, just as they recognized that Germanic culture was part of, and embedded in, broader Indo-European linguistic and cultural history, the Grimms were especially eager to emphasize the German qualities in the versions of stories they included in their collection.

The first scholarly theory about the origins of such tales as the Grimms', however, argued for the stories having come to Europe from India, partly because, as Jacob Grimm in his linguistic treatises had helped make plain, the European languages were related to India's ancient literary language, Sanskrit. If, as the Grimms themselves wished to believe, European folktale continued an ancient tradition of storytelling, then it was only reasonable to investigate surviving Indian texts for affinities with tales such as the Grimms'. The leading exponent of this theory of Indian origin was the German Sanskrit scholar Theodor Benfey, a younger contemporary of the Grimms, who expounded it forcefully in the introduction to his edition of the *Panchatantra* in 1859 (xxii): "my investigations in the area of fables, fairy tales, and tales of the East and West have [...] convinced me that few fables, but a great number of tales and fairy tales, have spread from India over almost the whole earth." Benfey conceived of the transmission of the tales as occurring both through oral and literary tradition, especially as regards Europe: "In European literature, the tales entered via Boccaccio, the fairy tales via Straparola. From literature they found their way into folk narrative again, etc., and achieved, particularly through the mutual activity of the national and the individual mind, that character of national truth and individual unity which endows many of the stories with such high poetical worth" (xxvi).

Benfey's thesis (see also his short essays, 1894), which inspired much or most of the research on folktale in the second half of the nineteenth century and came to be championed particularly by Reinhold Köhler (1894; 1898) in Germany and Emmanuel Cosquin (1922) in France, amounted to a theory of monogenesis, not only for individual stories but for European folktale as a whole. This extreme position regarding the question of origins was prominently opposed by the French philologist Joseph Bédier in his famous study of medieval merry tales, *Les Fabliaux* (1893). Bédier rightfully cast doubt on the soundness of the methods used by Benfey and other proponents of the thesis of Indian origin and contended that a case could just as well be made for polygenesis, or independent origins.

Bédier argued that the whole concern with the origins and paths of propagation of folktales was a fruitless endeavor that diverted attention from study of the stories themselves, as they were narrated in a given place and time. He was intent on viewing folktales as products of a particular ethnic culture. Scholars who attempted to trace stories to their origins were focusing on elements in the tales which rested, in the case of most merry tales, "on moral ideas so general that they can be equally acknowledged by everyone in whatever time," and in the fairy tales, "on marvels so ill-defined that they would not offend any belief, and could be equally accepted, as simple amusing fantasies, by a Buddhist, a Christian, a Moslem, and a Fetishist" (xviii-xix). It is therefore useless to try to determine where a given folktale originated (xx):

> We must the accept the polygenesis of tales. We must give up these sterile comparisons of versions that pretend to discover laws of propagation which can never be discovered because they do not exist. We must abandon these vain classifications which are based on the similarity, in different countries, of certain traits that are necessarily insignificant (by the very fact that they reappear in different countries)—and which neglect the local elements of these narratives that are markedly different and do not travel well, [that is, neglect] the only interesting things.

After Bédier, theories of monogenesis applied to European folktale as a whole met with sharply declining interest. Thus, the orientalist Alfred Forke (1911), in writing on "The Indian Folktales and Their Meaning for Comparative Folktale Research," generally agreed with Bédier that the stories typically were not from a single origin, but the result of polygenesis.

In connection with the thesis of Indian origin, another approach had arisen that sought to interpret folktales as conveying ancient mythological—especially meteorological—symbolism. The leading proponent of this theory was another German Sanskrit scholar, Max Müller. Müller, and other scholars who followed his lead, sought to connect the characters and events in folktale with the movements of heavenly bodies and with other natural phenomena. Their belief was that the stories were conceived originally as representations of such phenomena. For example, the prince's awakening of Sleeping Beauty was seen as depicting the sun's warming of the earth in springtime (see Bolte and Polívka, 1913-32, V: 253-256, for further discussion of this direction in folktale study).

The interpretation of folktale as symbolizing natural phenomena offered support for the theory of polygenesis, since this type of storytelling could easily have arisen in any primitive society. Anthropologists in England, including E. B. Tylor (1865; also 1871 and 1881) and James Frazer (1890), argued for the similarity of simple primitive myths the world over; and Andrew Lang (1887 and 1898) claimed that folktales could be traced to prehistoric times from which primitive elements, or "survivals," remained recognizable in the stories. Following Lang's lead, Pierre Saintyves (1923) in France interpreted folktales as depicting primitive ritual, so that Sleeping Beauty represented springtime's awakening and Bluebeard a ritual testing of the bride (for fuller discussion of the anthropological school of folktale study, see Bolte and Polívka, 1913-32, V: 256-257, and Thompson, 1946, 379-383).

While the rise of folklore as an object of scholarly interest owed much to the emergence of anthropology as an academic discipline, the formal, organized study of folktale as a field had its origins in nationalist sentiment. Patriotism, indeed, had played no small part in the Grimms' enthusiasm for folktale. At the time they began their collection, German-speaking lands were occupied by, or dominated by, France under Napoleon. One reason the Grimms provided notes to their collection was to suggest that the telling of such stories was widespread among German-speaking people. The existence of different versions of the same tale in different parts of Germany and by different storytellers would testify to the poetic creativity of the folk.

The beginnings of what became the international society for the study of folktale, the Folklore Fellows, had its origin in similar nationalist sentiment in Finland (this account of the beginnings of the 'Finnish school' follows that given by Thompson, 1946, 396). There, in 1835, Elias Lönnrot published a national epic, the Kalevala, based on collections of heroic ballads he had made. Lönnrot's disciple Julius Krohn, in carrying that work further, devoted himself to comparing all versions of a given song in the Kalevala cycle to determine its life history, analyzing the songs according to motifs, studying their geographical distribution, determining the migration of the song from one area to another, and characterizing the changes in the song that were made in the process. Krohn's son Kaarle applied this historical-geographical method to folktale, in a doctoral dissertation on Finnish stories about the involvement of a bear or wolf with a fox. The younger Krohn subsequently founded the international society for folktale study, which published the first of its long, still continuing monograph series Folklore Fellows Communications (abbreviated FFC) in 1907 (see Kaarle Krohn, 1907; 1931). The potential of folklore studies for enhancing national pride and patriotic spirit was evident; following Finland's lead, governments in other countries supported creation of folktale archives.

One result of the interest in folktale as a national phenomenon has been the creation of reference works for the study of the stories in a given country or language area, such as the catalogue for French-speaking countries by Paul Delarue and his collaborator Marie-Louise Tenèze (1957/1964) and the *Dictionary of British Folk-Tales in the English Language* by Katherine M. Briggs (1970/1971), the latter being actually a collection of stories—some only summarized—divided and classified in the manner of the Finnish school. Another result was the collecting of tales for specific national or geographical areas, following the model of the Grimms. Among the early examples of these was A. N. Afanasyev's collection of Russian tales (1855-1863); Joseph Jacobs's of forty-three English stories (1890/1894); for Germany, J. W. Wolf's collection (1851) as well as E. Meier's tales from Swabia (1852), and Samuel Singer's study on collections from Switzerland (1903/1906). Finally, in the twentieth century there have been a number of scholarly studies of stories from particular countries or language areas. August von Löwis of Menar compared the heroes in German and Russian tales (1912). Karl Spieß provided an introductory characterization of the German *Volksmärchen* (1917). Gianfranco D'Aronco (1957) published a descriptive and analytical bibliography of variants for the best-known or principal types of tales in Italy, with special attention to sources in classical mythology; and Felix Karlinger authored an introduction to the folk literature of the Romance language countries (1969), while Ursula Klöne (1961) studied the introduction of folktale into literary prose in Italy from Straparola to Basile. And Waldemar Liungman (1961) investigated the origin and history of Swedish folktales.

The origin of the international folklore society in national sentiment helps explain why the Finnish, or historical-geographical, method tended to avoid large claims about the source and meaning of European folktale as a whole, such as had characterized the study of folktale in the second half of the nineteenth century. What mattered now was to show which tale types were native to, or predominated in, a given area, so that a particular story might be claimed as belonging especially to a particular national culture. Or, in a comparative way, differences in versions between geographical areas could be seen as helping to define cultural differences between nations. To use a botanical analogy, while a particular plant may grow in various countries, it may flourish especially in a given geographical location, or the adaptations it has undergone in that region can help illustrate differences in climate. Since the Finnish method of folktale study arose during the course of the Darwinian era, it is perhaps not amiss to suspect that, consciously or unconsciously, the historical-geographical method modeled itself on biological science. Carl Wilhelm von Sydow (1948), for example, was concerned chiefly with the geographical distribution of tales, applying the term "oicotype" to versions native to, or characteristic of, a given area.

The historical-geographical method depends on being able to establish commonalities between stories in order to demonstrate which tales are of the same type, and which not, just as the botanist was concerned to identify the genus and species of plants. To this end, an index of tale types was created by Kaarle Krohn's disciple Antti Aarne (1910). In his preface to his application of this method to three folktales (1907), Aarne described the aim of this approach as follows (iii-iv):

> If we proceed from the assumption that folk fairy tales are stories which have arisen in a definite area and at a definite time, and have spread through borrowing from one land to another, from one people to another, and in doing so have changed and been recast [...], then we cannot characterize the search for the homeland of a story as effort expended in vain. [...] If we succeed in cleansing a tale of the changes and expansions it has suffered on its journey and if we discover the original form of the tale, then light has been shed therewith on the homeland of the tale and the paths it has traveled; and thus we possibly receive hints as well about the time of its origination.

(See also Aarne, 1913.) The index was later revised after Aarne's death by the American folklorist Stith Thompson (1928; for a listing of the categories, see Thompson, 1946, 481). Thompson explicitly recognized biological science as the model for his and Aarne's still standard classification: "Biologists long since have labeled their flora and fauna by a universal system and by using this method have published thousands of inventories of the animal and plant life of all parts of the world. In like manner it should be possible to make available for study the entire body of collected folk-narrative in the world" (1946, 413-14).

Defining the essential elements of a given tale type is no easy matter, however, except in cases where differences between versions are relatively minor. What Aarne did, in practice, was to set out the tale types largely with reference to the stories in the Grimms' collection, often even labeling a type with the title given to the tale by the Grimms. Since stories frequently share certain elements of plot, or motifs, without there being sufficient similarity on the whole to claim that the stories are of the same type, Stith Thompson proceeded to create, too, an index of folktale motifs (1932-36; see also Thompson, 1955).

Starting about the time of the appearance of the Aarne-Thompson index of tale types, other aids to the study of folktales (and folklore generally) began to be produced. Hanns Bächtold-Stäubli's ten-volume handbook of German superstition (1927-42) remains a standard reference work. The handbook of German folktale edited by Lutz Mackensen (1930-40) was never completed, but is being supplanted by the encyclopedia of folktale (*Enzyklopädie des Märchens*), begun in 1975 by Kurt Ranke and others and planned for twelve volumes. In English one may consult the *Funk & Wagnalls Standard Dictionary of Folklore, Mythology, and Legend* edited by Maria Leach (1949) and Gertrude Jobes's *Dictionary of Mythology, Folklore and Symbols* (1961-62).

The organizing of folktale studies as a scholarly discipline under the auspices of the Finnish school through its Folklore Fellows Communications coincided with the first book surveying the theory and history of this area of research, that by Adolf Thimme (1909). Thimme's handbook is still interesting as a reflection of the view held at that time concerning the development of folktale study since the Grimms. There followed Alexander Haggerty Krappe's *The Science of Folklore* (1930), which afforded the non-specialist a presentation of principles of folklore studies. Krappe championed the Finnish method—which he calls the Literary school—against that of the anthropologists. Basic to his argument is that folktales were invented for entertainment. More completely orthodox with reference to the Finnish school is the handbook by Stith Thompson, *The Folktale* (1946), which remains the standard general work on the subject in English. From an Italian perspective, there is Giuseppe Cocchiara's general history of European scholars' interest in folklore (1954), and in French Roger Pinon's introduction to the study of folktale as a science (1955). The best introduction in German to the scholarly study of folktale, including the history of that field's various aspects, is Max Lüthi's volume in the Sammlung Metzler series of handbooks (1962a), with its critical bibliography of secondary literature on the subject.

Contemporaneous with the establishment of the Finnish school of folktale study in the first decade of the twentieth century was the emergence of psychoanalytic theory, and with it, almost immediately, interpretations of folktale from that perspective. These studies at first reflected Freud's ideas. Less than ten years after his *Interpretation of Dreams* (*Die Traumdeutung*, 1900) there appeared Franz Riklin's early attempt (1908) to interpret fairy tale and myth as involving dreams of sexual wish-fulfillment. A decade later Otto Rank published his collected essays on the psychoanalytic study of myth (1919). And Alfred Winterstein contributed to Freud's journal *Imago* (1928) a lengthy essay on survivals in folktale of puberty rites for girls.

Folklorists and psychoanalysts were not the only furtherers of scholarly interest in folktale at the start of the twentieth century. Literary scholars, for their part, were concerned with questions such as distinguishing among folktale genres, especially between merry tales like those familiar from Boccaccio's *Decameron* and Chaucer's *Canterbury Tales*—the genre referred to in German as *Schwänke*—and what we call in English 'fairy tales' (in German, *Märchen*; the English term arose in connection with Charles Perrault's tales and especially those by other, female practitioners of the genre at the court of Louis XIV).

An early study on the distinction between merry tales and fairy tales was the 1904 dissertation by Ludwig Felix Weber. He offered the suggestion that fairy tales were products of the female imagination and merry tales creations of the male imagination, because the former revolved around erotic love whereas the latter did not (38-39). Moreover, in merry tales there is no "sharp distinction between beautiful and ugly." The women in these stories are "never the most beautiful in the world or as ugly as sin" (45), Weber's implication being that when it comes to storytelling women are more concerned with the issue of beauty than are men. Weber noted also that the term 'nursery tales' (*Ammenmärchen*) suggests that the tellers of this type of story were women, and he maintained that "all collectors [of such tales] got the most beautiful and characteristic pieces from the mouths of women" (64-65). Walter Berendsohn, in his Habilitationsschrift (1921), similarly argued for erotic love as the decisive characteristic of the fairy tale, defining the genre as "a love story with hindrances, and which ends with the eventual union of the pair of lovers" (35).

Like Weber and Berendsohn, Marie-Elisabeth Rosenbaum, in her dissertation (1932), characterized fairy tale as essentially a story of love and marriage, unlike the merry tale. Meanwhile, surely influenced by Freudian theory, Friedrich von der Leyen, one of the leading German literary scholars to devote himself to the study of folktale, had expressed the opinion that fairy tale's unique character was owing to its origination in dreams (1911). And Berendsohn somewhat similarly asserted that "the world of magic [in folktale] is a place for fanciful fulfillment of secret wishes and hopes that cannot be fulfilled in the real world" (1921, 35).

Other studies concerned with questions of genre, mostly by German literary scholars, aimed at distinguishing fairy tale (*Märchen*) from legend (*Sage*), as the Grimms had done already in publishing fairy tales (the *Kinder- und Hausmärchen* of 1812 and 1815) and German legends (the *Deutsche Sagen* of 1816) separately. An early study of this question in the twentieth century was that by Friedrich Panzer (1905), who claimed for legend a more realistical, serious, historical, and tragical world. Panzer also addressed the question of eroticism in fairy tale, making the point that in these stories "little is made of the erotic side of love" (12)—which is not to deny its underlying presence. To be sure, the Danish literary scholar and folklorist Axel Olrik (1909) focused on shared characteristics of folk narrative, seeking to identify its unspoken rules; but the dominant trend was to emphasize differences between the various genres. Thus, Hans Honti (1931) discussed the relationship between fairy tale and heroic legend, and suggested that ancient fairy tales (*Urmärchen*) could have been an important source of inspiration for the latter type of story. Konrad Tönges (1937) similarly viewed fairy tale as the oldest form of folktale, older than the merry tale or even legends, and argued that some *Märchen* originated in Germany no later than the Middle Ages. Max Lüthi (1943), by contrast, judged legend to be the more primitive genre, a creation of the folk, with fairy tale being the more artful, literary creation. Lüthi emphasized the fairy tale's qualities of artfulness, abstractness, and one-dimensionality in attempting (1943; see also 1947) to define and describe the *Märchen* as a literary form distinct from both legend (*Sage*) and pious tales (*Legenden*). Hermann Bausinger, too, concerned himself at length with the distinctiveness of fairy tale (1968) and, echoing Friedrich Panzer's comment given above, observed in a later study that while merry tales and jokes "sometimes approximated a fragmentary theory of sexuality [...] the fairy tale hardly ever exploits the basically erotic situation" (*die erotische Grundkonstellation*). While accepting Berendsohn's "classical short definition" of the fairy tale as a "love story with hindrances," Bausinger justifiably observed that in these tales "neither love nor the hindrances are portrayed in detail from the physical side" (1980, 62-63). The relation between legend and fairy tale and their ties to cultural history was the subject, meanwhile, of a number of essays by Lutz Röhrich, which he collected and published in 1976.

A major debate between literary scholars and folklorists arose in the 1920s and 1930s centering on the claim by Albert Wesselski (1925; 1931; 1938), a philologist, that folktale derived ultimately from literary works, not from oral tradition, and that fairy tales (*Märchen*) in particular were not older than the late Middle Ages or the Renaissance. Wesselski's argument for the subordinate role of oral tradition drew a rebuttal from the prominent Estonian folklorist Walter Anderson (1935). The debate was reviewed by Ernst Philippson (1945), a philologist teaching in the United States, and also by an American folklorist Emma Emily Kiefer (1947). Anderson addressed the issue again by publishing the results of an experiment (1951). A counter-experiment was conducted by Kurt Schier and reported on in his 1955 dissertation. Anderson then published a rebuttal (1956) to Schier's finding that stories are not well preserved as they are passed on in oral tradition and that their transmission is dependent on literary tradition.

A number of other critics have dealt in a broader way with the relationship between oral transmission and literary versions. In a series of essays (1950/51; 1952; 1954), Paul Delarue, the noted French folklorist, argued the case for the complementary role of oral and literary tradition in the transmission of folktales, with emphasis on the oral tradition and with special regard to Perrault's stories. Lutz Röhrich, in his edition of selected tale types as represented from the German Middle Ages down to modern times (1962/1967; see also Röhrich, 1956a), showed a connection between the literary and folk tales, particularly how certain tales written since about the mid-1200s became popular or survived. Röhrich granted that these tales may already have belonged to popular storytelling before they first appeared in literary form—or more precisely, before their first-known literary appearance—but he emphasized the close connection between popular storytelling and short narrative genres that had been established in literary tradition no later than the early Middle Ages.

An Italian scholar meanwhile, Sebastiano Lo Nigro (1964), focused on the creative element in oral transmission, stressing the important role the storytellers' own nature and involvement plays in how the stories are told. Each teller has a characteristic style, which at the same time seeks to preserve the tradition, that is, to tell the stories essentially as they, the storytellers, have heard them. Lo Nigro contended that the best tellers are those who emphasize the human and realistic aspects of the story, however magical or wondrous the events may be. In this way, he pointed to a middle ground on the issue of oral versus literary transmission: each storyteller is a poet in his or her own right.

The extent to which the manner and point of storytelling depends on the authors, their times, and their cultures was considered, too, by Felix Karlinger in his introduction to the literary evidence for the existence of folktale tradition in the Romance countries (1969; see also Wetzel, 1974), from the earliest records in the Middle Ages down to the folklorists' collecting of oral tales—an activity that essentially did not begin until the second half of the nineteenth century. Placing the collections of tales by Basile and Perrault in the context of this development, Karlinger concluded that before those collections (i.e., before the seventeenth century) there were no true fairy tales, at least not of the sort we have come to understand by that term. Like Lo Nigro, Karlinger maintained that "the teller tells the story the way *he* himself has grasped and understood its meaning and unity" (1969, 16; Karlinger's emphasis).

Testimony to the close relationship between oral and literary tradition has been given, too, by Rudolf Schenda (1983, 79) in connection with his editorship of the multi-volume *Enzyklopädie des Märchens*, every new fascicle of which indicates afresh that countless tale types and motifs were drawn from the treasure trove of medieval epics and lives of the saints, from Renaissance novellas and humanist compilations, from Baroque sermons and Enlightenment doctoral dissertations, from almanacs and chapbooks. We have read far too little of the vast amount of these 'lower' literary genres to be able to maintain that some form of 'oral' tradition was not written down or printed and read or read aloud and thereby transported further along, either shortly before it or at most two generations before the storytelling act.

Schenda's point is thus that oral tradition is likely to derive from literary tradition and vice-versa, with literary tradition playing perhaps the leading role in preserving the stories.

What folklorists, justifiably, are unwilling to accept is that a literary version of a tale be considered authoritative with regard to a given story type. As a leading contemporary American folklorist, Alan Dundes, has argued (1986, 261), "When one studies the Perrault or the Grimm text of a fairy tale, one is studying a single text. This may be appropriate for literary scholars who are wont to think in terms of unique, distinctive, individual texts written by a known author or poet. But it is totally inappropriate for the study of folklore wherein there is no such thing as *the* text. There are only texts."

For critical and interpretive purposes, folklorists want to study types of tales, not individual stories. Dundes describes the procedure as follows (1986, 266):

The folkloristic approach to fairy tales begins with the oral tale— with literary versions being considered derivative or secondary. It includes a comparative treatment of any particular tale, using the resources of numerous publications and the holdings of folklore archives, as indicated in the standard tale-type indexes. Ideally, the folkloristic approach should incorporate a healthy eclectic variety of theoretical orientations which would be more likely to reveal the richness of the fairy-tale genre, its symbolic nature, and its enduring fascination.

Lutz Röhrich, meanwhile, has further complicated matters by pointing out that what a story means differs not only according to who is telling it but who is listening, and indeed at what point in their lives (1984, 3): "Fairy tales and legends are like a mirror: everyone sees his or her own face in them, that is, something of his or her own personality. From narrator to narrator and from listener to listener a single story can have vastly different meanings. The meaning of a story can even change for an individual in the course of his or her life, in that, while the objective meaning of a text may remain the same, the personal meanings change." Röhrich thus adds the subjective reception of tales to the individuality and creativity of the tellers, to which Ludwig Felix Weber (1904, 64) had pointed almost a century before in addressing the question of authorship: "For no folktale can we name an author. [...] we must insert the last teller in place of the unknown author. In the end both are after all the same, for the creator is only the first in the ranks of the tellers. But every succeeding teller performs anew a sort of act of creation; he does not transmit the tale like the copier of a manuscript."

Because of the interaction between oral and literary tradition in the transmission of folktales, many in this area of study have perceived a need for collaboration between folklorists and literary scholars. Karl Spieß (1917), soon after the emergence of folktale studies as a distinct discipline defined by the Finnish school, emphasized the importance of combining folkloristic and literary methods, the latter being seen as especially important for the question of meaning in given historical contexts. The same point was made a decade later by Helmut de Boor (1928), who urged that the philological approach to texts be made a component of the study of folktale, as did Carl Wilhelm von Sydow (1948) in his essay on "Folktale Research and Philology" (*Märchenforschung und Philologie*; both DeBoor's and von Sydow's essays were reprinted in the volume *Wege der Märchenforschung* edited by Felix Karlinger [1973]).

De Boor criticized the Finnish geographical-historical method for its "conscious forgoing of the study of fairy tale (*Märchen*) as a literary genre," which meant that the ultimate result of this research always failed to go beyond determination of the "origin, propagation, and transformation of the individual narrative materials and types." Such results have no more meaning for understanding texts than, for example, "the working up of a complicated manuscript genealogy for a literary work or the tracing of a literary theme through its different reworkings in world literature." The Finnish method's "necessary emphasis on motifs [...], the isolation of the single narrative elements from one another, leads to the not insignificant danger that concentration on the parts will result in forgetting the whole, indeed in altogether abandoning the tale as a unified artistic work and seeing in the motifs the actually essential element" (1928, 144). Similar concerns were voiced two decades later by von Sydow, who argued that "collaboration between philology and folklore studies is of the greatest importance [...]. The study of folktale must orient itself toward investigations which are important to others than just specialists in the field—first of all, naturally, to philologists, whereby, as mentioned, as close a collaboration as possible must occur" (1948, 192).

Another direction in folktale studies that developed in the early decades of the twentieth century was the structuralist approach, as advanced by the Russian scholar Vladimir Propp. Propp (1928) attempted to provide a model of the sequence of narrated functional elements that identified a fairy tale (*Märchen*) as belonging to that genre. Shortly after, a similar attempt, but more closely related to earlier philological notions of genre, was made by the literary scholar André Jolles (1930), who set about to define the "form" not only of *Märchen*, but all other familiar types of folk or popular narrative as well. The studies by Propp and Jolles were followed by many others attempting a definition or description of folktale genres. Wilhelm Giese's *Zur Morphologie der Märchen der Romanen* (1932), despite the reference to "morphology" in the title, took no note of Propp's study, and used instead a more conventional approach, focusing on formulaic elements characteristic of *Märchen* as a particular folktale genre. Werner Spanner's *Das Märchen als Gattung* (1939), too, followed a traditional approach to fairy tale as a genre, as Jolles had done. In succeeding decades, Jolles's type of inquiry continued to characterize these studies, including Max Lüthi's *Das europäische Volksmärchen: Form und Wesen* (1947), Jan de Vries's study of fairy tale in its relation to myth and heroic legend (1954) and his much earlier *Het Sprookje* (1929), and Kurt Ranke's critical survey (1958) of the literature on the functionality of the various narrative genres represented in folktale and the special place of fairy tale therein. Karl Justus Obenauer's approach (1959), too, was of a general literary sort, not formalistic in a theoretical sense like Propp's.

A decidedly literary approach to the question of genre was that of Ursula Klöne (1961), who investigated the introduction of fairy tale into the Italian novella, following that development from Boccaccio through Straparola to Basile, with other examples along the way. In Basile's *Pentamerone*, fairy tale had supplanted the novella as the primary form. A similarly oriented study was undertaken by Hermann Hubert Wetzel (1974), who attempted to discover survivals of fairy tales from oral tradition in the French novellas of the Renaissance, Wetzel's argument being that in this period *Märchen* came to be frowned upon in favor of the more realistic novella and that fairy tales as such had existed already in the Middle Ages.

Most studies on folktale genre have continued to address the question in the manner of Jolles or Lüthi. Leopold Schmidt's *Die Volkserzählung: Märchen, Sage, Legende, Schwank* (1963) was of this type, as was Hermann Bausinger's *Formen der 'Volkspoesie'* (1968). Lüthi himself, though, while adhering basically to study of form in a traditional sense, evidenced a shift (1975) toward a philosophical concern with the image of man as depicted in folktale.

A contrary example is the Proppian analysis undertaken in Illana Dan's "Attempt at a Model for the Surface Level of the Narrative

Structure of the Female Fairy Tale" (1977). Propp's theory, which remained little known until after World War II, was the basis, too, of such later studies as Steven Swann Jones's structuralist analysis (1983) of the Snow White tale. Jones modified Propp's theory as follows: "a different typological pattern underlies each different tale type, not simply one structural pattern as Propp suggests. [...] Thus, folk narratives appear to be structured in two ways: The typological structure characterizes the action consistently found in the different versions of the same story, while the generic structure describes action commonly undertaken in different stories" (57). Heda Jason (1986) also approached the question of genre in folk literature from a structuralist viewpoint, while Yigal Zan argued that the goal of structural research should be "the *illumination of the ultimate meaning of the given folktale* or [...] the identification of the most likely idea for whose communication a given folktale was composed" (1989, 229; Zan's emphasis).

Manifestly political coloration of folktale studies occurred, expectedly, in Hitler's Germany. In a dissertation of 1937, Wilhelm Jürgens attempted to accommodate folktale to Nazi ideology by applying Heideggerian terminology to *Grimms' Fairy Tales* and thereby to find them to be an expression of the soul of the German race (Jürgens's subtitle refers to "the ontology of mythical consciousness"). Josef Prestel's pedagogically oriented commentary on the Grimms' stories addressed to schoolteachers (1938) similarly related fairy tale to Germanic mythology—and to heroic legend—with the avowed intention of linking the stories to the cultural and moral history of the German race, without however actually advocating racism or supporting Nazism as such. A connection with Nazi ideology is indicated, too, by the title of Will-Erich Peuckert's study of German folkways (1938) that appeared in a series of the same name; but Peuckert's title, in referring also to "Fairy Tale and Legend, Merry Story and Riddle," suggests at the same time relevance to the discussion of folktale genres to which Propp and Jolles had given new impetus in the previous decade.

Following World War II, in the period of the 'Cold War,' literary criticism on the Continent tended to reflect the political division of Europe into East and West, with existentialism as the dominant philosophy in the 'free world' and Marxism the imposed ideology in the Communist countries. Neither existentialist nor Marxist critics in this postwar period displayed great interest in folktale, however, though there were exceptions. Helmut Birkhan's Vienna dissertation (1961) on transformations in fairy tale was, for example, from an existentialist viewpoint. The new approach in the postwar years came rather from the psychoanalytical camp, and indeed now from the Jungian direction, whereas earlier the way had been led by Freudians.

Among the first Jungian approaches to folktale was that taken by Joseph Campbell in his since much acclaimed book *The Hero with a*

Thousand Faces (1949). Its counterpart on the Continent was Hedwig von Beit's three-volume *Symbolik des Märchens* (The Symbolism of Fairy Tales, 1952-57). These early Jungian interpretations were followed then by two studies by psychiatrists, Julius E. Heuscher's *A Psychiatric Study of Fairy Tales* (1963) and Hans Dieckmann's interpretation of oriental tales from the standpoint of "depth psychology" (1966); by the series of volumes of lectures by Marie Louise von Franz (1970; 1972; 1974; 1976); and by Sibylle Birkhäuser-Oeri's study of the "mother- complex" in fairy tale (1976). These were not the very first Jungian studies, however. They had been preceded by those of Wilhelm Laiblin on the primeval image of the mother (1936) and on the symbolism of salvation and rebirth in the German folk fairy tale (1943; see also his later, 1956 essay on the symbolism of transformation) and by the—albeit only vaguely psychoanalytical—book by Marguerite Loeffler-Delachaux on symbolism in fairy tales, the latter having appeared the same year (1949) as Campbell's hugely influential treatise.

A view similar to the Jungians' in its positing of an importance of fairy tale for the human unconscious was expounded by the well known historian of religion Mircea Eliade. In an essay on folktale scholarship (1956), Eliade maintained not only, as some earlier scholars had done, that fairy tales had their origins in rites of initiation common in earlier cultures, but that modern hearers and readers of fairy tales unconsciously experience such initiation: "While modern man believes that, in reading fairy tales, he is entertaining himself or escaping from reality, he unconsciously is succumbing to the influence that the initiation is exerting on him in the guise of the fairy tale. One could assume that fairy tales very quickly became a gentler imitation of [...] rites and mysteries and that they had simply the function of recreating the initiatory tests on the level of dream and fantasy" (1956, 318).

The surge in Jungian interest in folktale, which served to attract attention to the genre among psychoanalytic critics generally, brought in its wake a Freudian study that was to make the interpretation of fairy tales a matter of much broader debate among the general educated public, particularly in the United States. With the publication of Bruno Bettelheim's *The Uses of Enchantment* (1976), Freudian theory regained its original dominance in the psychoanalytical study of folktale. Like most psychoanalytical commentators, Bettelheim was concerned with what folktale shows about growing to sexual adulthood and to maturity and with the lessons about this process contained in the stories. In particular, he focused on the therapeutic effect folktales may have on children as they experience the process of maturing.

Bettelheim's findings in many ways echoed those of an earlier Freudian study, Bruno Jöckel's *Der Weg zum Märchen* (The Pathway to Understanding Fairy Tales, 1939) that had appeared—rather astonishingly—

under Hitler in the year of Germany's invasion of Poland, though both the author and the publisher were presumably Jewish and the regime was quite eager to suppress discussion or application of psychoanalytical theory. Jöckel's study deserves to be better known, for its interpretations are more easily convincing than many advanced by Bettelheim. While Jöckel's book is not so very readily available in academic or other libraries (presumably owing to the time and circumstances of its publication), an essay of his that had been published in the postwar years (1948) did achieve a measure of prominence through its inclusion in the anthology of psychoanalytical criticism of folktale edited by Wilhelm Laiblin (1969). In *The Uses of Enchantment* Bettelheim oddly cited neither Jöckel's book nor that essay.

Another Freudian study preceding Bettelheim's was that by Günther Bittner on the symbolism of female maturation in fairy tale (1963). Meanwhile, from a somewhat different psychoanalytical perspective, Erich Fromm discussed the interpretation of fairy tales in his *The Forgotten Language* (1957). And a psychiatrist, Ottokar Graf Wittgenstein (1965) related twenty-five of the better-known tales to the problems of his patients, taking an approach less indebted to Freud or Jung than to ideas of Martin Buber, such as the importance of "I-Thou" relationships.

The importance of psychoanalytical criticism in folktale studies since World War II is reflected in publications discussing that approach. Gabriele Leber's essay (1955) distinguished between the ideas of the various schools of psychoanalytical theory as regards their applicability to folktale. Wilhelm Laiblin's anthology of essays on 'depth psychology' and folktale research (1969) demonstrated the rise of the psychoanalytic approach dating from Freud's *Interpretation of Dreams* at the start of the twentieth century, and showed the reaction of folklorists and literary scholars toward this development. Then Hans Eberhard Giehrl, the following year, published a survey of psychoanalytic studies on folktale for schoolteachers (1970) in which, while not advocating this approach, he expressed appreciation of its possible contributions (as might be expected in a book published for schools in Catholic Bavaria, Giehrl is less critical of Jung than of Freud). Max Lüthi, in his short handbook (1962a), had likewise been willing to accord this approach a place in folktale studies: "The psychoanalytical interpretation of fairy tales has in the twentieth century come into similar disrepute as had the mythological interpretation toward the end of the nineteenth century. Yet the psychoanalytical interpretation remains an important complementary contribution to the interpretation of *Märchen*" (83).

Bettelheim, in his day the leading authority on autism in children, came to fairy tale by way of his interest in developmental psychology. A similar interest has led many critics, beginning early in the twentieth century, to find pedagogical meanings in folktales. Moreover, beginning no later than with Perrault's *Tales of Mother Goose* at the end of the seventeenth century, fairy tales had been considered—at least as a poetic pretense—to be stories for children. Studies of folktale as children's literature, however, did not appear until over two centuries later, after the emergence of psychoanalytic theory, which offered theoretical models for explaining the pedagogical import of these popular stories. Perhaps the first such book-length study, that by Charlotte Bühler, appeared around the end of World War I as a supplement volume of the *Zeitschrift für angewandte Psychologie* (Journal for Applied Psychology). Erwin Müller's essay on dream and fairy-tale fantasy appeared (1930) in the *Zeitschrift für pädagogische Psychologie* (Journal for Pedagogical Psychology, 1918). Similarly, Josephine Bilz's study published during World War II (1943) came out as a supplement volume to the *Zentralblatt für Psychotherapie* (Central Organ for Psychotherapy); and Agnes Gutter's book, a quarter of a century later (1968), appeared in the series "Arbeiten zur Psychologie, Pädagogik und Heilpädagogik" (Studies on Psychology, Pedagogy, and Therapeutic Pedagogy). Meanwhile, Bühler's pioneering study had been republished, together with excerpts from that by Bilz, the latter now titled "Märchengeschehen und Reifungsvorgänge unter tiefenpsychologischem Gesichtspunkt" (Fairy-Tale Happenings and Processes of Maturation from a Depth-Psychological Point of View; Bühler and Bilz, 1958, 73-111).

These and other pedagogical studies, in viewing folktales as often depicting a process of maturation, did not do so within the framework of psychoanalytic theory as such, however. Bühler's book (1918) was rather a somewhat empirical attempt to explore fairy tales as children's literature, especially children's reactions to the stories. Müller's 1928 dissertation on the psychology of the German folktale was a non-psychoanalytic evaluation of fairy tales' appropriateness for children. Bilz (1943), too, took the approach of a more general developmental psychology, as opposed to that suggested by psychoanalytic theory. While Gutter (1968) did not ignore the role of sexual development, her concern was with the process of growth and maturity in a broader, moral sense, and with the symbolic depiction of that process in folktale. Christa Federspiel (1968), like Bühler a half-century before, addressed the question of which types of tales appeal to children and took an empirical approach, not a theoretical one. Ortrud Stumpfe (1965), meanwhile, in seeing the stories as pedagogically therapeutic, approached the symbolism in folktale rather more idealistically or platonically than psychoanalytically. The studies referred to above are all by scholars from the German-speaking countries. There followed soon, however, an example of such pedagogically oriented criticism in England, Elizabeth Cook's

volume (1969) published by Cambridge University Press and sub-
titled "An Introduction to Myths, Legends, and Fairy Tales for Teachers
and Storytellers."

More analytically oriented was the volume edited by Siegfried
Schödel (1977), an anthology of excerpts from interpretive literature
on folktale that presents a broad spectrum of views, as a basis for
critical discussion in secondary school classrooms. Also, Max Lüthi,
in some of his publications (1956; 1969; 1975a; 1977), addressed his
reflections about fairy tales to teachers and the broader public. And
Peter Wolfersdorf published a similarly oriented study for teachers
(1958) entitled "Fairy Tale and Legend in Research, the School, and
Youth Work." Finally, though the title gives no hint of it, Walter
Scherf's dictionary of magical tales (1982) viewed the stories as
depicting developmental psychology, to which Scherf refers as
"finding the way to one's self" (*zu sich selbst finden*), but in a more
mystical than psychoanalytical sense.

A form of idealistic approach to folktale, yet with affinities to
Jungian theory, is that of the anthroposophists. The founder of this
religious-philosophical movement himself, Rudolf Steiner, showed
the way with lectures in the pre-World War I period in which
(1908/1913) he claimed that folktale helps reveal the depths of the
human soul and thereby also the spiritual nature of the universe.
Steiner's disciples subsequently followed suit, an early one being
Rudolf Meyer (1935). More recently, Friedel Lenz (1971) interpreted
a number of the Grimms' most famous tales from this viewpoint, as
did Edzard Storck (1977), who in his preface acknowledged indebt-
edness to Meyer and Lenz. While Storck, seeing folktale as depicting
a process of spiritual development, wrote of "childhood in God as
the forming of the heavenly human being," a decidedly Christian,
as opposed to anthroposophist, approach is found in the book by
Arland Ussher and Carl von Metzradt (1954), where some of the
better-known Grimm stories are interpreted as representing arche-
typal human experiences as understood by Christianity, not by
Jungian or anthroposophist theory.

The beginnings of a sociological, as opposed to psychological or
spiritual, approach to folktale reach back to the 1920s, with the publication of Hans Naumann's introduction to folklore as a science
(1922). Like the anthropologists, Naumann considered folktales to
contain survivals from earlier times. The fairy tales (*Märchen*), as
distinguished from legend (*Sagen*), he viewed, however, not as
products originating in popular culture, but as cultural property of
the upper levels of society that had filtered down to the common
people—as being "gesunkenes Kulturgut." The common people re-
produce, instead of producing, the latter being the function of the
ruling classes. Naumann's theory anticipated Albert Wesselski's
subsequent contention (1925; 1931; 1938), discussed earlier, that oral

folktale derives from literary tales and not the other way around. Like Naumann, Wesselski maintained that folktale originated with the educated classes.

Alongside the sociological perspective on folktale there developed an ethnological approach, which studies the influence of cultural differences on storytelling. Gédéon Huet's presentation of folktale for the general reader (1923) emphasized the particular cultural origins of the folktales. Writing in Germany under Hitler, Will-Erich Peuckert, in his study (1938) referred to earlier, argued that there was a specifically German handling of common European folk narrative, and that each culture adapts these genres in its own way (Peuckert's view that there is a specifically German "bearing" [Haltung] in that culture's versions of the tales would appear to echo a theme from Nazi ideology). Vladimir Propp, too, used an ethnological and anthropological approach (1946) in applying to questions about the historical origins of folktale the structural method of analysis he had developed in his earlier study (1928). In the post-World War II years Anneliese Dymke, in a Würzburg dissertation (1951), displayed a more cosmopolitan orientation, undertaking a comparative study of variants of stories with an eye to historical and national differences, and concluding that how a story is told indeed depends greatly on the culture and the times. Similarly, Lutz Röhrich, in his Habilitationsschrift of 1956, found the origins of folktale to lie in the believed realities of the given culture, and emphasized that the story as a whole, not just isolated motifs, must be examined in this regard. Röhrich viewed European folktale as containing survivals from an archaic period. The renowned French anthropologist Claude Lévi-Strauss, too, in advocating structural analysis of myth (1955), was out to uncover the cultural beliefs and concerns underlying various versions of the same story, as was Leopold Schmidt in his subsequent study (1963), who considered folktale to date from the bronze and iron ages and argued that one must attempt to understand the stories as they were understood within the society and culture in which they were told. And Liliane Mourey's comparative study (1968) of the Grimms' tales and those of Perrault adopted the French structuralist viewpoint. The importance of cultural context in the reception of folktales was emphasized anew by Röhrich in his 1984 essay: "The meaning of a text is not a fixed constant but is a variable, determined by the development of culture and ideas, fashions and trends, and dependent on rules and ruling ideologies, not to forget the education and cultural awareness, the age, sex, religion, and ethnic group of the consumer" (2).

A corollary of Röhrich's comment is that storytellers tailor their tales to their audiences. Linda Dégh (1962) studied oral tradition in Hungary as an example of how storytelling is affected by the shared culture of the teller and audience. Dégh, though, also stressed the individuality displayed by the tellers' adaptations of their material. Richard Bauman, a leading advocate of the study of folktales as oral performance, has similarly argued that "A [...] noticeable consequence of our deeper awareness of the artfulness of oral literature and the radical importance of performance as constitutive of verbal art has been the restoration of the work of oral literature to the creative individuality of the performer's accomplishment" (1986, 3; see also Bauman, 1978, 4). Dégh, Bauman, and other folklorists have been interested in storytelling as a performing art; two other books, by Charlotte Rougemont (1962) and by Vilma Mönckeberg-Kolmar (1972), however, concerned the different matter of recitation of tales from written texts, an art of which they themselves were practitioners.

Another social scientific approach was taken by August Nitschke, who attempted to place folktale in social and cultural contexts as viewed from the perspective of behaviorism. Like the anthropologists, Nitschke in his two-volume study (1976/1977) saw popular narrative as having its origins in primitive, preliterate, prehistoric times; but his aim was to investigate folktale's changing function down through the ages within cultures and societies, in so far as that function can be documented.

Still more recent has been the effort to show how class struggle, as understood in Marxist theory, has affected the transmission and literary adaptation of folktale. Prominent among these critics has been the American Germanist Jack Zipes, beginning especially with his *Breaking the Magic Spell: Radical Theories of Folk and Fairy Tales* (1979), and continuingly reflected in his subsequent books on the subject (1983a; 1983b; 1986). Zipes is concerned above all with the transition from folktale to literary fairy tale, and on to utopian literature, science fiction, and related genres in the mass media of the twentieth century. His view is that popular tales were inspired by visions of an ideal social order. As he put it in the preface to *Breaking the Magic Spell*, the tales "sought to celebrate humankind's capacity to transform the mundane into the utopian as part of a communal project" (1979, ix).

An approach similar to Zipes's had been used a bit earlier by Dieter Richter and Johannes Merkel in their book *Märchen, Phantasie und soziales Lernen* (Fairy Tale, Fantasy, and Social Learning, 1974). Richter and Merkel analyzed literary folktales as having been adapted to serve the pedagogical aims of the emerging bourgeoisie. From their Marxist perspective, they assumed that actual folktales (*Volksmärchen*) tended to reflect feelings and dreams of oppressed masses under the feudal system. Their study's ultimate aim was pedagogical in a Marxist sense: to restore to folktale something of this assumed original spirit, and therewith an awareness of social issues and problems and an early habit of thought about social reform and emancipation of the oppressed.

Oppression based on gender, not class, has been the focus of feminist criticism of folktale, which arose in connection with the women's movement that got underway in the 1970s. Among the early examples of this type of study was Marcia Lieberman's essay (1972/1973) "'Some Day My Prince Will Come': Female Acculturation through the Fairy Tale." Lieberman complained, with regard to the implicit message for women, that in many of these tales courtship "is magnified into the most important and exciting part of a girl's life, brief though courtship is, because it is the part of her life in which she counts most as a person herself. After marriage she ceases to be wooed, her consent is no longer sought, she derives her status from her husband, and her personal identity is thus snuffed out" (394). As Lieberman's title indicates, she had in mind not only folktales as such, but especially also Walt Disney's cinematic versions of some of the most popular stories. In an essay that soon followed, Kay Stone commented wittily on the passivity of Disney's heroines, even when compared with those in the Grimms' versions of the stories: "if the Grimm heroines are, for the most part, uninspiring, those of Walt Disney seem barely alive" (1975, 44). As Stone went on to note, justifiably, "the popularized heroines of the Grimms and Disney are not only passive and pretty, but also unusually patient, obedient, industrious, and quiet. A woman who failed to be any of these could not become a heroine." A broader, balanced verdict on the issue of female passivity, though, was given by Rosemary Minard, in the introduction to her collection of stories *Womenfolk and Fairy Tales* (1975, viii): "for the most part, female characters, if they are not witches or fairies or wicked stepmothers, are insipid beauties waiting passively for Prince Charming. There are, however, fairy tales which do present their women as active, capable, and courageous human beings." This latter sort of story, "The Fairy Tale of the Active Heroine," was investigated from a structuralist point of view by Heda Jason (1984).

To counter the depiction of the folktale heroine as passive, as waiting only for marriage, "with no power over her fate and no active involvement in choosing or planning the circumstances of her life," Ethel Johnston Phelps published an anthology of stories in which "all the heroines, in one way or another, take on active roles and make decisions to shape their lives. [...] Out of the few surviving [folk]tales that give us true heroines, we have selected a gallery of strong, delightful women and girls for readers of all ages to enjoy" (1978, xxi). Likewise, in a second anthology (1981), Phelps aimed to "portray spirited, courageous heroines" (xi). In introducing the first of the two anthologies, she raised the issue of whether it was desirable that "all heroines are extremely beautiful" since "for many children, it is discouraging to read this." She suggested therefore that "Although elements of extraordinary beauty [...] are an integral part of some plots, in many tales these are embellishments that can be dropped without affecting the story." Regarding the depiction of older women, Phelps protested, with reason, that "There is a marked pervasiveness of older women as frightening hags or evil crones" and that there "are too few surviving tales of likeable old women" (1978, xx).

Phelps's implied claim that in earlier times stories with positive portrayals of older women were more frequent found explicit expression in Heide Göttner-Abendroth's study that posits the origin of magical folktales (*Zaubermärchen*) in a prehistoric matriarchal society (1980, see 133-71). Göttner-Abendroth speculated that the heroines in certain of these tales were "originally magically powerful princesses" who later came to be portrayed as being "half children," as in the Grimms' versions of Sleeping Beauty, Cinderella, and the Frog Prince (170). Much the same opinion, and at the same time, was voiced by Ruth Bottigheimer in her essay "The Transformed Queen: A Search for the Origins of Negative Female Archetypes in Grimms' Fairy Tales" (1980, 12): "In my estimation the many fairy tales involving the wooing and winning of a princess [...] are remnants from [...] ancient belief in the powers of women."

The question of magical folktale's origin in prehistoric matriarchal societies aside, feminist criticism emphasized that folktales as we know them are the product of a culture in which status and power were in men's hands. Thus, Karen Rowe argued, in her essay "Feminism and Fairy Tales" (1979, 239), that the stories "are not just entertaining fantasies, but powerful transmitters of romantic myths which encourage women to internalize only aspirations deemed appropriate to our 'real' sexual functions within a patriarchy." From this viewpoint, the—conscious or unconscious—intent of the storyteller or adapter is to teach behavior deemed appropriate by a male-dominated society. Rowe maintained, *"Because* the heroine adopts conventional female virtues, that is, patience, sacrifice, and dependency, and *because* she submits to patriarchal needs, she consequently receives both the prince and a guarantee of social and financial security through marriage" (246, Rowe's emphasis). More recently, a similar discussion was offered by Linda Dégh about career choices for women in folktale (1989).

From a Marxist perspective, feminist criticism may be seen in a broader context of social protest. Jack Zipes commented that (1986, xi), in demonstrating that "the illusions of traditional fairy tales [...] have been structured according to the subordination of women," the feminist fairy tale "in speaking out for women also speaks out for other oppressed groups." Zipes is referring here to feminist adaptations or rewritings of traditional fairy tales, or to such stories as created by feminist writers. The feminist and Marxist perspectives also have in common that, in particularly strong contrast to

Bruno Bettelheim and other psychoanalytical critics, they seek to
place folktale in an historical context. Zipes, for example, maintained
(1983a, 47) that in contributing to "the literary 'bourgeoisification'" of
folktale, the Grimms "wanted the rich cultural tradition of the common
people to be used and accepted by the rising middle classes." From
a non-Marxist perspective Robert Darnton, an historian, adopted a
similar viewpoint (1984) with regard to Perrault's version of Little
Red Riding Hood. Lutz Röhrich, meanwhile (1986c), comparing the
images of women in the Grimms' tales with those in folksongs they
had collected but never published, likewise agreed that these depictions strongly reflect the patriarchal society of the times. Similarly,
Michele Rak (1986), in his edition of Basile's *Pentamerone*, studied
that work in the context of the literary and social culture of its day;
while Barbara Broggini (1990) also undertook to view Basile's career
as a poet in relation to the society of his place and time. And Marina
Warner (1990), from the perspective of women's studies, pondered
the image of the old woman as teller of tales. Most recently, my
study *Fairy Tale Romance* (1991), too, attempted to place the tales in
their historical context even while focusing, like the psychoanalysts,
on the stories' depiction of erotic psychology, a subject Lutz Röhrich
(1986a) briefly discussed with more specific regard to cultural and historical contexts.

An historical orientation has been reflected, too, in studies focusing on the vogue of fairy tales in the eighteenth century. As Charles
Deulin long ago observed (1879, 11), before Perrault the stories were
referred to in France as either "Tales of Mother Goose" (*Contes de ma
mère l'Oye*) or by the heroine of one such tale, "Peau d'Âne," as
being especially representative of the genre as a whole (perhaps
significantly, that tale starts out with a father's mad wish to marry
his daughter). The vogue of fairy tale in Perrault's own day was
studied by Mary Elizabeth Storer (1928). Gonthier-Louis Fink more
recently (1966) investigated the arrival and progress of that French
vogue in Germany. And most recently, Manfred Grätz, having
searched in vain for evidence of an oral tradition for fairy tale in
Germany before the time of the Grimms, concluded (1988) that there
was none, so that in Germany at least, the literary vogue led to oral
telling of the tales, not the other way around.

Useful bibliographies on folktale studies have been compiled,
especially since the 1930s, when research and criticism on popular
narrative had begun to emerge as a distinct scholarly field. Among
the early bibliographical aids were those of Friedrich Ranke (1936)
for the years 1920 to 1934 and Lutz Röhrich (1955-57; 1956b) for the
post-World War II period, together with the anonymously published bibliography (1946/49-49, 1952) for items that appeared in
the German Democratic Republic and Herta Uhlrich's list of publications (1959) for the years 1956 to 1959. Since that time, an annual

bibliography has been published in the journal *Fabula*. Among the volumes of collected essays on folktale, the anthology by Felix Karlinger (1973) in the series Wege der Forschung (Pathways of Research) is of particular importance, together with the earlier volume in that series by Wilhelm Laiblin (1969) on psychoanalytical approaches to folktale referred to above. The more recent volume of essays edited by Helmut Brackert (1980), in the series 'edition suhrkamp,' provides a sampling of rather more radical approaches that have arisen beginning in the 1970s.

2: The Grimms' Collection

SCHOLARLY COMMENT ON GRIMMS' FAIRY TALES, like that on folktale generally, begins with the Grimms themselves. In the prefaces to the editions of their folktale collection, and in the notes to the individual stories, Jacob and Wilhelm established perspectives and lines of inquiry that have provided subjects of debate in scholarship on their folktale classic down to the present. We shall therefore begin by surveying the issues raised by the Grimms' prefaces and their notes.

The Grimms' preface to their original volume (1812) begins by asserting that the stories are remnants of "the wealth of German poetic literature in early times," the implication being that much of what once belonged to poetic tradition on a grand or 'national' scale was preserved only in "popular song, and [in] these innocent household tales" (1986, v-vi). Several issues are raised immediately by this claim. One is whether these stories were German in origin, or at least to what extent they could or could not be claimed as products of the poetic imagination of that people. A second issue was whether the stories were remains of a sophisticated poetic culture or imaginative creations of the common folk. A third, related question is the degree of 'innocence' shown in the tales. Were they products of an adult or a childlike imagination?

The second paragraph of the preface touched on further matters that would occupy scholars studying the collection. The Grimms told of their initial belief that the number of such surviving stories was limited, and that they would find little more than differing versions of tales already familiar to them at the start (vi). Here they pointed importantly to wide variation in the way the same story was told and thereby raised, by implication, such questions as the faithfulness of transmission in this type of oral tradition and how variants of one and the same story are to be identified as such. In going on to report that by "asking about very widely" they found many more stories than they expected and that these were tales "collected according to oral transmission" (vi-vii), the Grimms provided several other issues for scholars: how many informants did they actually have and how widely scattered were they in "Hessia and the regions of the Main and the Kinzig [=a tributary of the Main] in the county of Hanau, where we are from" (vii); how faithfully did they record tales from oral sources; and did they have the tales from these sources directly or from informants who had written them down for the Grimms?

Although the Grimms reported finding more stories than they thought they would, they also made reference to a decline in the number of storytellers: "those who are supposed to preserve them [the stories] are becoming ever more rare." Storytellers were perhaps not common but "those who still know them [the stories] also know rather many" (vii). Scholars have since concluded that the Grimms' direct sources from oral tradition were few indeed. The question has also been raised as to whether the telling of such stories as the Grimms included in the collection was ever widespread. Was such storytelling relatively rare in the Grimms' time because it had actually never been common?

Other important issues are raised by the Grimms' claim that the tales are characterized by a childlike purity (viii). Together with their prior reference (vi) to the stories' 'innocence,' this claim implies that the tales are devoid of irony, satirical humor, and the like. But were the stories created for children? What was the intended audience? Are the Grimms' own stories characterized by an innocent tone? Are some and some not? Is such innocence pretended? Is innocence, even if only pretended, characteristic of the genre in general, or only as the Grimms conceived of it? Do these stories appeal to adults by recovering for them a measure of childhood naiveté?

In their first preface, the Grimms also took a position on whether the stories have a moral, in the sense of something to teach. Their answer was that while "from these fairy tales a good teaching, an application to the present, yields itself so easily," providing such a moral is "neither their purpose nor were they invented for that reason" (xii). The Grimms' view, then, was that the stories were not didactic in a narrower sense. At the same time, they indirectly invited their readers to discover lessons to be learned from the tales. That invitation, in turn, has helped encourage critical debate about what the stories teach, if anything.

Subsequent scholarly discussion on distinguishing between fairy tale (*Märchen*) and legend (*Sage*) found impetus, too, in this first preface. The Grimms explain the difference between the two genres as being that "the actually *local popular legends*" are "bound to physical places or to heroes of history" (xiii, the Grimms' emphasis), implying that fairy tales are not fixed in this way with regard to geographical location or time and are therefore better adapted to wider transmission through oral tradition.

Regarding the tales' age, a subject that likewise came to be a major scholarly concern, the Grimms believed that "their basis must be very old" even though "over the passage of time they have constantly created themselves anew" (xiii-xiv). Here the question poses itself as to how stories' possession of a common "basis" is to be determined, for purposes of designating one tale as progenitor of another. Still more problematical was the Grimms' assigning of age to a story based on occurrences of names, motifs, and the like in myth and legend, since these items do not insure that a particular fairy tale actually existed at such time. Can evidence of this sort be substituted for survival of the text of a story itself?

The Grimms' preface makes the point, too, that storytelling is common to all cultures: "there is probably no people that does without it [=this poetry] entirely" (xiv). Here was an implied invitation to scholars to test the truth of this assertion, and also to ask as to differences in the types of narrative between cultures. The Grimms recognized the existence of a common body of tales shared by the peoples of Europe, "so that a kinship among the noblest nations reveals itself in them [=in the stories]" (xv), as the Grimms' presumptuously remarked vis-à-vis non-European cultures. At the same time, the Grimms raised the issue whether these stories had not originated in the German-speaking countries, when they referred to "the great diffusion of these German [tales]" (xv). Such a comment encouraged the belief that the stories were originally German, and then inevitably also the question as to whether there was any evidence for that belief. The Grimms similarly suggested that northern Europe was rich in such popular narrative with "the southern countries perhaps less so" (xv), though they also made prominent mention of Charles Perrault's tales (xvi-xvii) and admitted that "richer than all the others are older Italian collections, first of all in Straparola's *Nights* [...], but then equally in Basile's *Pentameron* [...]" (xvii).

The Grimms' discussion of Perrault's tales bears on the much-debated issue of faithfulness to oral tradition, and therewith the question as to the characteristics of oral fairy tales. The Grimms praise Perrault for having "treated them [the tales] still as stories for children" and "not added anything and, small matters aside, left things unchanged" (xvi). At the same time, the Grimms were well aware of the influence of French linguistic culture upon Perrault's narrative: "his presentation deserves praise as being just as plain as it was possible for him" considering that "probably nothing is harder [...] for the French language in its present form [...] than to be naive and direct" (xvii). Finally, the Grimms' discussion of Perrault mentions an assertion, in the preface to an edition of the latter's tales, that "Perrault first invented them [=the stories] and through him [...] they first became disseminated among the folk" (xvii). The Grimms, of course, rejected this view; but we see here an anticipation of later scholarly debate as to whether the stories originated in oral or in literary tradition.

In view of the Grimms' praise of the simplicity of Perrault's stories, it is surprising that they were favorably impressed by the style in Basile's tales, which they rightly characterized as "overflowing with good talk and sayings" (xviii). The reason for that approval was surely the Grimms' interest in folk expressions, which came to be reflected in Wilhelm's insertion of them into tales in later editions. Since the Grimms viewed occurrence of folk expressions as a mark of authenticity, they did not consider their addition to be an adulteration of the texts but restoration of them to something closer to an imagined original form.

When the Grimms proceed, in their preface, to describe their own transmission of the stories, they implicitly leave room for stylistic additions and changes. They say only that they "have been concerned to understand these stories as clearly as possible" and that "No circumstance has been added by way of poetic invention or been prettified or altered" (xviii). In particular, they set their procedure apart from that of earlier literary transmitters of folktale, who "almost always used them as material for making larger tales out of them, which [were] arbitrarily enlarged and changed" (xix). The Grimms also raised the issue of 'literary contamination'—later much discussed with regard to their own collection—when they complained about literary transmitters of folktale who "just could not refrain from mixing in mannerisms provided by the poetry of the times" (xix). The Grimms observe, though, that simply the need to retell the stories in "a refined written language" (xx) robs them of much of their charm, and by implication, their authenticity as oral tales in a narrower sense.

With their preface to the second volume of their tales (1815), the Grimms insisted still more strongly that the stories were native to the German-speaking lands. They referred to connections between German heroic legends and the Low German stories they now had from Westphalia through literary friends there (the aristocratic Haxthausen and Droste-Hülshoff families), and to those from a peasant woman of their acquaintance in Cassel as being "genuinely Hessian" tales (1986, iii-iv). Above all, the Grimms now asserted that "they [=the stories] [...] put a new light on our ancient heroic poetry" (vi) and, more extravagantly, that "in these folk fairy tales there lies sheer primeval German myth" (vii). Indeed, the Grimms urged further collecting of such stories "to help lay a foundation for the scientific study of the origin of our [German] poetry" (viii).

In this preface of 1815, the Grimms similarly identified their collection more closely with oral tradition, by describing the storytelling manner of their new 'Hessian' informant, Frau Viehmann from the village of Zwehrn near Cassel. The Grimms emphasized that "She preserves these old legends firmly in her memory" (v). The Grimms' use of *Sagen* here instead of *Märchen* was perhaps meant to suggest that the two genres share a common ancient German origin, just as their report that the woman "in repeating [a story] [...] never changes anything materially" (v) implies that the tales have remained essentially the same in oral tradition over the centuries. The claims for the connection between German fairy tales and German heroic legend and myth and for the degree of faithfulness in oral transmission of tales were to become subjects of heated debate for later scholars. Regarding the equally important question of what the Grimms meant by faithfulness to oral tradition, they do not go so far as to claim that Frau Viehmann changed not a word from one telling to the next, only that she did not change matters of fact.

A new, later much debated issue was raised in the 1815 preface as well. The Grimms referred to criticism that if their collection is intended for children, as educational material ("ein eigentliches Erziehungsbuch"), things should be omitted that are "embarrassing and inappropriate for children, or offensive" (viii). The Grimms' response was that the stories should not be censored because "everything can be wholesome which is natural" (ix). They argued that great popular classics always contain "such matters for scruple," among them first and foremost the Bible; yet "proper usage will not discover anything evil, but only, as a beautiful expression says: a witness to our heart" (ix-x). The question for scholars has been: did the Grimms—even in their first edition—live up to this implied claim not to have bowdlerized their tales?

The Grimms take a position, too, on the meaning and significance of differing versions of stories. They speak against the assumed existence of "an actual, at one time extant original form" of a story in favor of viewing the versions as "on the contrary, possibly only attempts to approximate, following manifold paths, an inexhaustible [primal form] that is present only in the mind" (x). In other words, the 'true' story exists only as an idea, with any given version being merely an attempt at its realization (that the Grimms lived in the—heavily platonic—period of German philosophical idealism is evident here). For later scholarship, the issue of determining which version of a tale is the more authentic became a major preoccupation, including the question of the existence of ideal forms of the stories. Which version is best turns on the issue of what one believes the story ideally should be.

At the conclusion of their 1815 preface, the Grimms reaffirmed their assertion that their tales were "purely German and not borrowed from anywhere" (xi). In doing so, they made a further point relevant to subsequent scholarly criticism. Since the Grimms were intent on arguing that the tales are ancient, they commented that in determining when and where a story originated, it is not sufficient to point to incidental matters in the text: "since precisely these things, after all, like the words in today's speech, change form according to the tellers' way of speaking, and one can count on it with certainty that in the fifteenth century they [=the tellers] put in mercenaries and rifles instead of soldiers and cannons [...]" (xi). Specifically, the Grimms were addressing themselves to the criticism that their tales were not really German, but borrowed "from Italian, French, and Oriental books" (xi). While the brothers certainly acknowledged— and indeed commented elsewhere on—the deep similarities between their stories and those found in Basile, Perrault, and the *Arabian Nights*, they evidently wished to believe, nonetheless, that their tales were older and that the borrowing, if any, had been the other way around.

The Grimms combined, and considerably revised, their prefaces to the volumes of 1812 and 1815 to create a new preface for the second edition of their collection (1819). While they continued to maintain their opposition to "an anxious elimination of things that refer to certain conditions and relationships as they daily occur and can in no way remain hidden," they did admit to bowdlerizing their texts to the extent of having "in this new edition carefully removed every expression inappropriate for children" (1980, I: 17). The Grimms reported also having "almost entirely revised" the first of the two original volumes with an eye to making the tales more complete, better, "simpler and purer" (21). Identifying and analyzing such removal of 'inappropriate expressions' and other changes between the first and second editions became an important subject for scholars in the twentieth century, as they sought to understand how the Grimms viewed their mission as tale collectors and editors.

In their new preface, which served for the collection as a whole, the Grimms continued to claim German origin for their stories, as can be seen in their report that they had "once again checked everything that seemed suspicious—i.e., what might have been of foreign origin or falsified through additions—and then eliminated everything [of that sort]" (21). Referring again to the Hessian origin of many of their stories, especially those in the first volume, they maintained that Hessia, being a "mountainous" and out-of-the-way place devoted primarily to agriculture, had "the advantage that it can better preserve old customs and traditions" (20). Later, scholars would check for themselves the Grimms' claim of German—and specifically Hessian—origin for their stories.

Related to the question of origin is that of faithful transmission, on which the Grimms had touched in their original prefaces. Now, in the new preface, they elaborated on this point, probably in response to skepticism about their fidelity to their sources. They confessed to having used their own judgment in editing the material. In particular, they were concerned to eliminate whatever they believed was not authentic: "attentiveness, and a tact which one acquires only with time, is necessary in order to distinguish between that which is simpler, purer, and yet more complete in itself from what has been falsified" (21-22). As they also made clear, when more than one version of a story was available to them, they had to decide which variants to blend together as the version to be included in the collection: "We have communicated different tales as a single tale, in so far as [these versions] complemented one another and, in order to combine them, no contradictions needed to be eliminated; but whenever [the versions] differed, wherever each then had its own peculiar characteristics, we gave preference to the best [versions] and saved the others for the notes" (22). Scholarly critics have been left to discover, as best one can, what principles guided the Grimms in deciding about the authenticity of their material as folktale and in choosing among versions of the same tale, especially in deciding which—often composite—version to include and which to relegate to the notes.

After the Grimms elaborated on their handling of their sources, they concluded their new preface with an expanded protest against revising or adapting folktales by inventing or adding material not found in the stories as transmitted. In making this protest, however, the Grimms showed awareness that in oral tradition storytellers may use their own poetic imaginations: "To be sure, it is without doubt that in all living feeling for a work of poetry there lies a poetic forming and re-forming without which transmission itself would be something barren and withered; just this [forming and re-forming] is part of the reason why every region, in accord with its peculiarity, [indeed] every mouth narrates differently" (22-23). Where the Grimms draw the line is when the intrusion of literary sophistication becomes evident. For them, the mark of authentic folktale is that "the spirit of the people dominates in the individual [storyteller] and does not allow particular desires to push to the fore," whereas for identifying literary sophistication "The single guideline would be then the poet's presently prevailing intention, which is dependent upon the [storyteller's] education" (23). The Grimms' concern with authenticity was not owing, though, simply to their wanting to believe that folktale was an expression of a communal poetic spirit, but to their belief that folktale preserved information about ancient times: "If one concedes scientific value to these transmissions, then it is self-evident that through such revisions this value is almost always destroyed" (23). Here the Grimms again identified an issue that would subsequently occupy scholars: how does one distinguish between oral tradition and the literary folktale?

Another concern the Grimms expressed in the preface of 1819 was that literary versions of the tales would take the place of traditional versions in storytelling. At least, this fear seems to lie behind their complaint that "every revision of these legends (Sagen) which removes their simplicity, innocence, and unpretentious purity tears them from the province to which they belong and where, without causing boredom, they are desired [to be heard] ever again" (23). The Grimms expressly exclude actual literary fairy tales from this condemnation: "this is said [...] only against so-called adaptations which intend to prettify the tales and endow them with more poetry, not against a free conceptualization of them for particular poetic works that belong entirely to their own time" (24). To be sure, the Grimms' prejudice in favor of folktale is obvious in the implication that the latter is immortal while literary fairy tales are not. Yet they were right in so far as literary fairy tales, in the narrowest sense, have indeed failed to become immortalized through oral telling, but have remained stories to be read. The question here that has occupied scholars has been, rather, the extent to which the stories in the collections by Perrault and the Grimms—which strove especially to realize an ideal of fairy tale as folktale—influenced oral storytelling in France and Germany, and beyond.

The Grimms' prefaces to the five subsequent editions—those of 1837, 1840, 1843, 1850, and 1857—were far briefer than the preface of 1819, because that preface to the second edition was reprinted in each following edition, as were each of the succeeding prefaces in turn. These succeeding prefaces had simply the function of updating the preface of 1819, largely just reporting changes in the collection made between the new edition and the preceding one.

The preface to the third edition (1837) reported that, aside from adding "a number of new tales appended to the second part" of the collection, in order "to bring [it], as far as possible, closer to completeness," "many of the earlier pieces have been revised once again and supplemented and enriched through additions and certain features obtained from oral tales" (1980, I: 24). It is noteworthy that the Grimms do not actually claim that the "additions" in the texts are from oral tradition, only "certain features" among the changes they have introduced. This indirect admission bears on the question subsequently asked by scholars as to which changes were of the Grimms' very own invention and which from oral or literary sources.

The preface of 1837 also assertively reiterates the Grimms' conviction that their tales' display of "some surprising relationships to ancient legends of the gods" and of "agreements with nordic myths" serves as "proof of the original connection" between the tales and myth and legend (26). Scholars are left to decide whether, as the Grimms' claim, their tales are of ancient origin, like myth and legend, or only certain individual themes and motifs are very old, while the Grimms' stories themselves are of more recent provenience.

The Grimms contributed further to the impression that their tales were from oral tradition in the brief preface to the fourth edition (1840), where Wilhelm singled out from among the tales they had added one from their home area that "a peasant from Zwehrn told to one of my friends" (1980, I: 26). Wilhelm's comment that one sees therefore "that wisdom in the street has not entirely perished" suggests, however, that finding oral tales was not so very easy. Scholars would later point out that the Grimms increasingly turned to published sources in adding to their collection.

While the preface to the fifth edition (1843) raised no issues of subsequent importance to scholars, the following preface (1850) brought Wilhelm's report that he had been "continuously [...] striving to introduce [into the texts] folk sayings and characteristic ways of speaking, for which I am always listening" (1980, I: 27). His use of this editorial practice poses the question whether or not he was taking inappropriate liberties with the texts, since it is suggested that his sources were too lacking in the use of folk sayings and expressions to suit his notion of how folktales should be.

The preface to the seventh edition (1857)—the last during the Grimms' lifetime—once again pointed to the issue whether their tales were actually German in origin. There they reported that a few stories had been dropped which they had discovered to have "arisen on foreign ground" (1980, I: 27).

Alongside the seven editions of their whole collection, the Grimms published a selection of fifty tales. In that anthology, as they noted in the preface to third edition of the whole collection (1837), "the concern of those is taken into consideration who do not think every piece in the larger collection is appropriate for children" (1980, I: 26). This selection for children, as it were, was understandably a greater publishing success than was the whole collection. In the preface of 1837, the Grimms reported that in the years between the larger collection's second (1819) and third (1837) editions, the shorter anthology, first published in 1825, had been reprinted twice (1833 and 1836); and in the 1843 preface to the large collection, they reported two further reprintings of the anthology (1839 and 1841; there followed editions in 1844, 1847, 1850, 1853, and 1858, for a total of ten editions during the Grimms' lifetime). Scholars are left to ponder such questions as why the Grimms chose as they did for this anthology, and what modifications, if any, they introduced to render the chosen stories appropriate for children.

Beginning with their notes to the first edition (1812, 60 pages in rather small print; 1815, another 70 pages), the Grimms made their own contribution to scholarship on the tales, and indeed therewith provided a model for folktale study as a whole. The notes reflect their 'scientific' concern—Jacob's particularly—to discover connections between Germanic mythology and German folktale. Each of these connections made in their notes invites scholarly scrutiny as well as a search for further such parallels or similarities. A famous case in point is the Grimms' association of the wall of thorns surrounding Sleeping Beauty (in their "Dornröschen," *KHM* 50) "with the slumbering Brünnhilde who is encircled with a wall of flames" (1986, I: xxxi). Yet the Grimms were interested, too, in such similarities between their 'German' tales and those in collections from other countries, like Basile's from Italy and Perrault's from France, because they were fascinated as well by the existence of some tales across cultural boundaries.

Since the Grimms wanted to claim their tales as German, they did not squarely confront the question of whether the stories came to Germany by way of Italy and France. This issue soon became an important one for scholars, not least because the Grimms themselves, in their notes, had shown wide connection between their tales and broader European storytelling traditions. Regarding Sleeping Beauty, for example, the Grimms noted not only the connection between their German version "Little Briar Rose" ("Dornröschen") and Perrault's "La Belle au bois dormant" (from which the English name for the story is taken), but also with Basile's "The Face" ("Lo Viso," *Pentamerone*, III, 3), where instead of a spindle the danger, as the Grimms noted, lies "with a dangerous bone" (1986, I: xxxi).

Another issue raised by the Grimms' notes is whether mere mention of a tale's name, or that of a person in the tale, in earlier literary works represents probable proof of the story's having existed already at that time. Regarding the first tale in their collection, The Frog Prince ("Der Froschkönig," *KHM* 1), for example, the Grimms claim that story must be meant when the sixteenth-century German author Georg Rollenhagen "names [the story about Iron Henry] [...] as being among the old German household tales" (1986, I: i), even though in the Grimms' tale the character in question has only a minor role at the end, a role some critics justifiably have labeled as superfluous. Nor is it convincing, with regard to how old a story is, when the Grimms go on to document, in earlier literature, the existence of expressions about iron bands around the heart referring to feelings of care and sorrow, like those of which Iron Henry speaks in the Grimms' Frog Prince. The question should be the other way around. When unusual or otherwise interesting expressions and images occur in folktale, we may want to know how far back in literature they can be traced; and this is indeed the question to which the Grimms' notes help provide answers. The Grimms' position regarding motifs as evidence of a given tale's age is clearer and readily acceptable. Concerning the story The Fisherman and His Wife (*KHM* 19), the Grimms remark, "The motif of the woman who spurs her husband on to higher rank is certainly ancient, from Eve [...] up to Lady MacBeth" (xi). No claim is implied that the occurrence of this motif proves the Grimm tale in question goes back per se to the Fall of Man, though that Biblical story surely played a role in the tale's invention.

A related question posed for scholars by the Grimms' notes is whether variant versions can be termed the 'same' story when differences in the telling produce differences in the meaning, or at least shed new light on the meaning. For example, the Grimms report for their second story, "Cat and Mouse in Company" (*KHM* 2), a version in which it is instead a rooster and a hen (1986, I: iv-v), so that the tale in this case is about relations between the sexes instead of between species of animals, though it is still about trust, deceit, and appetite. Certainly, accepting the proposition that the two stories are of the same type, as we may do in this case, is not to claim that the subject or meaning of the two versions is entirely the same; the matter depicted in some cases may indeed be entirely different. We can say that we have the 'same' story, but that some versions may have differing points or meanings.

In the expanded version of the Grimms' notes, which they published as volume three (1822) of their second edition and republished in 1850 and—revised and expanded—again in 1856, little or nothing new was introduced in the way of issues to be examined by later scholars. The Grimms did, however, more fully address the question as to how the same or similar tales could be found in different places (1980, III: 416). Their answer allowed for the possibility of both polygenesis and monogenesis. On the one hand, "There are [...] situations that are so simple and natural they the recur everywhere, just as there are thoughts that come to people as though all by themselves; therefore, in vastly different countries the same tales, or at least very similar ones, can be produced independently of one another" (405). On the other hand, the Grimms found that "in most cases, the particular, often unexpected, indeed capricious execution" of the tale "will have taken on a form that does not permit the assumption of a merely apparent relatedness" (405).

As the Grimms formulated the question of monogenesis: "How is one to explain it when the tale in a lonely Hessian mountain village agrees basically with an Indian or Greek or Serbian tale?" (406). Their answer was that this agreement was explained by these peoples having shared a common Indo-European origin, which the Grimms termed "Indo-Germanic" as "one is used to calling" it (423). The Grimms implied that among these related peoples, the German-speaking countries were the original, or most important, source since they maintained that "the relatedness [of the tales] circumscribes ever narrower rings around the areas settled by the Germans" (423), and that "Among the peoples of German stock, eagerness to preserve the tales has shown itself to be the most active" (416). The Grimms' answer, therefore, to how one could "find among the Arabs a few tales related to the German ones" was that the *Arabian Nights* had its origins in Indian sources (423), whereas the tales of the North American Indians and those from other non-Indo-European sources displayed no such close kinship indicative of monogenesis (424).

The revised and much expanded edition of the Grimms' notes done by Johannes Bolte and Georg Polívka in five large volumes (1913-32) did not raise much in the way of new issues. Bolte, assisted by Polívka chiefly for Slavic sources, confined himself, as he said in the preface to the first volume, largely to indicating "very briefly the content of many variants" that had been found since the Grimms' 1856 edition of their notes and to "providing solely a survey of the geographical diffusion of the individual narrative material and its traces in earlier centuries" (I: v-vi). That is to say, he continued the work begun by the Grimms, making it fuller and more systematic. The result was that this revision became—and remains—the standard edition of the notes for literary scholars and folklorists alike. Just as the Aarne-Thompson index directs scholars to other versions of a given tale type, the Bolte-Polívka notes show where, up to Bolte's time, versions of each of the Grimms' tales had been found.

Bolte did, however, add a history of the Grimms' collection (IV: 419-87) and a brief survey of "Theories about the Origin and Diffusion" of the tales (V: 239-64) which called attention to important questions for scholars. In his history of the Grimms' collection, Bolte repeated information that Wilhelm Grimm's son Herman had published (in 1897, in his essay "Die Brüder Grimm und die KHM") about contributors of tales, who in the Grimms' notes had not been specifically identified—information that was gleaned chiefly from the notes Wilhelm Grimm had written in by hand in his own copy of the first edition (1812, 1815; now available in the 1986 facsimile edition by Heinz Rölleke). With the provision of this information, it had become clear that the Grimms' immediate informants were generally not common folk, but indeed cultured friends of theirs.

In his essay, Herman Grimm observed that his father and his uncle did not publish the stories in the form in which they had received them. He commented, for example, "As a young girl my mother told the story of Hansel and Gretel to my father, to be sure; but that he just wrote it down as she dictated it to him—the matter here is not all that simple" (237). Moreover, Herman Grimm pointed to the information in the Grimms' notes to the collection as showing "how much both selecting and summarizing work, as well as editing, was necessary in order to arrive at that form for the tales in which the *Children's and Household Tales* became a collection which appears to have sprung ready-made from the mind of the German people" (238). For Herman Grimm, clearly, the form lent to the stories by the Grimms was a literary achievement, a judgment that came to be emphasized by scholars increasingly over the course of the twentieth century. Herman Grimm's essay, though, led scholars astray for over half a century regarding the identity of one of the most important contributors, whom he erroneously identified as "Old Marie," a war widow who lived in the house of Wilhelm

Grimm's eventual in-laws, the Wild family (240). Herman did, at the same time, note correctly, however, that the mother of the Hassenpflug daughters—including the actual "Marie," who was then still quite young—was "of French origin" (242), so that some of the stories the Grimms had from those girls showed influence from France.

Bolte's history also called attention (IV: 453-57) to the issue of the Grimms' treatment of their sources and their revision of their texts, which Hamann (1906), Tonnelat (1912), and others had investigated. Bolte commented on the Grimms' striving—particularly Wilhelm's—to achieve optimal versions of the stories: "The more numerously variants of one and the same tale came their way, the more urgent became for them the task of producing the purest and richest basic form from the different individual transmitted ones" (IV: 453). Bolte also pointed to Wilhelm's effort "In the structure as well as in the [manner of] expression to approach the ideal of a popular tale appropriate for children" (V: 453), and also to "weave expressions, similes, and sayings into the transmitted presentation" and to enliven the story through substitution of "soliloquy or dialog" for indirect speech (IV: 454). Bolte concluded, "All this repeated further shaping shows how little Wilhelm Grimm felt constrained by the form in which popular storytelling had conveyed the tales to him; the form [in which the stories were published] was his own free [intellectual] property" (IV: 457).

With the discovery of a manuscript containing the tales as the Grimms had collected them by the fall of 1810, and the publication of that manuscript by Franz Schultz (1924), a new area of scholarly investigation was opened. Now these manuscript versions could be compared with those the Grimms had published afterwards in their first edition of 1812. The manuscript's discovery was all the more important because the Grimms did not save notes or manuscripts for the tales that they included in their published collection. This manuscript survived only because the Grimms had sent it, toward the end of October, 1810, to their literary friend Clemens Brentano at his request. Brentano never returned it; and it found its way from among his posthumous papers to the library of the Trappist monastery in Ölenberg in Alsatia (the Grimms had made a copy of the manuscript for their own use before sending it to Brentano). Assuming that the versions of 1810 were closer to what the Grimms had from their oral sources, here was evidence for studying how they handled those sources in preparing their tales for publication. At the same time, the manuscript's discovery posed the prior question of how close the versions in the manuscript were to what the Grimms actually heard from their informants.

The literary shaping of oral folktales had already been the subject of a study in 1922 by Franz Heyden, who discussed this art as practiced by the Grimms themselves, as well as by two of their literary sources, the eighteenth-century German author Heinrich Jung-Stilling, from whose autobiographical novel *Heinrich Jung-Stillings Jugend* (1777) the Grimms had their tale "Jorinda and Joringel" (*KHM* 69), and by their Romantic contemporary, the painter Philipp Otto Runge, in his two contributions to the Grimms' collection, "The Fisherman and His Wife" (*KHM* 19) and "The Juniper Tree" (*KHM* 47). Far from aiming at censure of the Grimms for embellishing their oral sources, Heyden was intent on demonstrating their skill, and that of Jung-Stilling and Runge, as contrasted with the Grimms' chief competitor, Ludwig Bechstein, whose collections *Deutsches Märchenbuch* (1845) and *Neues deutsches Märchenbuch* (1856) rivaled theirs for popularity.

Further impetus to study of the Grimms' treatment of their oral sources was given by the new edition of the 1810 manuscript by Joseph Lefftz (1927), a more dependable, scholarly one than Schultz's had been. The new edition's appearance was followed by the Frankfurt dissertation of Elisabeth Freitag (1929) comparing the stories in the first edition of 1812 with the versions of them in the manuscript. Freitag considered the changes found in the 1812 edition under five main categories: 1) those made for greater clarity and vividness, 2) those for approximating folkways of speaking and narrating, 3) rectification of grammatical errors and avoidance of dialectical idiosyncracies, 4) adaptations to render the tales suitable for children, and 5) reworking of sources with an eye to external and internal form. Among the stylistic changes cited by Freitag were addition of alliteration, repetition of words, onomatopoeia, direct speech, and diminutives. She pointed also to increased attention to depicting household matters and life's material needs, as well as less open mention of sexual matters, elimination of vulgar expressions, and a greater role for prayer and piety. She noted as well the Grimms' special attention to the titles they gave the stories, particularly to help distinguish tales from one another. Freitag concluded that the Grimms' tales need to be seen as reflecting an intimate combining of the qualities of a collector with that of a poet, the spirit of a philologist with that of a creative artist.

In the case of a few tales, the manuscript of 1810 has not remained the only evidence for changes made by the Grimms in the stories as they may have first received them from oral sources. In his essay on "new original versions of the Grimm tales" (1953), Wilhelm Schoof compared tales as found in letters from Jacob Grimm to his scholarly mentor Friedrich Karl von Savigny from 1808, when the Grimms had only recently begun collecting *Märchen*, with subsequent versions in the 1810 manuscript or the 1812 first edition. Among these stories were better known ones like "The Holy Virgin's Child" (*KHM* 3), "The Wedding of Mrs. Fox" (*KHM* 38), "Little Snow White" (*KHM* 53), and "Rumpelstiltskin" (*KHM* 55).

Schoof cited the changes made in the Snow White story as especially illustrative of Wilhelm Grimm's "striving, with rhetorical techniques of every sort—particularly through sticking in lines of rhyming verse, expanded depictions, intensifications of motifs, and much else—to go beyond folk art and sophisticated art to create a classical fairy-tale style, without thereby altering the actual content" (88)—the latter claim being dubious, to say the least.

Among those questioning the Grimms' faithfulness to oral tradition was the East German scholar Gunhild Ginschel, in her book on Jacob Grimm's early years (1967). In addition to considering the extent to which their tales are reconstructed or embellished, Ginschel was out to discover whether Jacob and Wilhelm differed on how to proceed in this regard. She concluded that they were in essential agreement. Concerning the issue of eroticism in folktale, Ginschel found that the Grimms tended to soften the depiction of sexual matters so as to adopt an "unerotic posture" in the telling of the stories. In this connection, Ginschel called attention to the debate between the Grimms and their literary friend Ludwig Achim von Arnim about the meaning of the animal tale "The Wedding of Mrs. Fox" (*KHM* 38), in which the presumed widow will marry only a fox who has nine tails like her dear departed husband. Wilhelm was willing to admit that Arnim's interpretation equating tails and penises was possible (*Schwanz* = tail or penis, the former being the literal meaning of the Latin). Jacob, though, wished to believe in the tales' innocence, in the face of Arnim's contention (which the latter claimed was based on first-hand experience with storytelling among common people) that folktales were often astonishingly priapic—a quality which Arnim found to be ultimately natural and healthy. Ruth Michaelis-Jena, writing about "Oral Tradition and the Brothers Grimm" (1971), admitted that the Grimms turned the stories into "tales to be read," but judged that while "This undoubtedly meant a loss of [...] the genuineness the brothers had originally aimed at," the revisions, however, "made Grimms' Fairy tales a world classic" (266-67).

Still greater attention to the Grimms' relationship to oral sources was occasioned by Heinz Rölleke's publication (1975) of a new, improved scholarly edition of the manuscript of 1810, this time with the corresponding texts from the first edition of 1812 on facing pages. Most importantly, Rölleke offered a scholarly apparatus capable of serving as the basis for a new history of the Grimms' collection, especially as regards its origins and early stages. His notes on the identifiable contributors to the collection drove home the point that none of these sources fit the Grimms' ideal type of an elderly story-telling woman of humble rural origins (390). Thus Rölleke noted that Dorothea Viehmann, whose portrait appeared on the title page of the second edition (1819) and to whom Wilhelm

Grimm devoted the whole third paragraph of the preface as being an example of this type, was in reality a tailor's wife descended from a French Huguenot family who had grown up speaking French and was fifty-seven years old when she served the Grimms as an informant. Moreover, the earliest contributors to the collection were also from the urban middle class and, as a rule, of partly French-speaking or Swiss descent. Rölleke therefore concluded that the by then century-old French literary vogue of the fairy tale or *conte*, dating from Perrault, Marie d'Aulnoy, and others during the reign of Louis XIV, had a much greater and relatively more direct influence on the tales collected by the Grimms than they and a majority of German literary historians had perceived or, certainly, admitted. As regards the fate of the Grimms' copy of the 1810 manuscript and the manuscripts of the other stories they included in the collection, Rölleke judged that the Grimms presumably destroyed them to prevent unwelcome comparisons between the original versions and their reworkings of them (1974b, 332; see also 1978b).

Alongside studies of the Grimms' treatment of their oral sources, there has been similar increased interest in this question regarding the other two classic literary collections of fairy tale, those by Basile and Perrault. Whereas for the Grimms' collection the discovery of the 1810 manuscript offers some idea of what certain of their tales were like as received from oral sources, for Basile's and Perrault's stories there is no evidence at all of the form in which those authors may have had them from oral tradition. Nevertheless, Paul Delarue (1954), in reviewing the question of Perrault's authorship of his tales, contended that the stories, as Perrault's title page suggests, were indeed written down by his young son from an oral source, but were then reworked, augmented, and readied for publication by Perrault himself. Marc Soriano, in his critical study (1968a) of Perrault's tales applying biographical, folkloristic, and literary perspectives, chiefly addressed the question of the extent to which Perrault was faithful to putative oral tradition, and especially how and why he made presumed changes. Similarly, Giovanni Getto (1964) investigated the style and content of Basile's tales—his whole manner of storytelling—as a product of the Baroque age's mentality and atmosphere, as has been done more recently by Michele Rak (1986), in this case with particular attention to the literary culture of Basile's place and time.

Related to the Grimms' handling of oral sources is the question of changes they made in their tales' style and content from their first edition through the seventh, the last published before their deaths. Reinhold Steig (1901) had early maintained that "the fairy tales and the legends, in truth, were created by the Grimms in literary fashion, as though by poets" (277) and that the Grimms' models for their ideal fairy tale form, the two stories contributed by Philipp Otto Runge ("The Juniper Tree," *KHM* 47, and "The Fisherman and His Wife," *KHM* 19), "were both written with the most purely artistic of intentions" (280). Hermann Hamann (1906) studied the changes introduced by the Grimms in stories they had from literary sources—that is, printed versions to which they had access—including also, to some extent, changes they made in these stories in subsequent editions. Hamann concluded that while the content was changed very little, the form and style often was, as the Grimms developed a new narrative tone. He noted, too, that in the case of one tale (*KHM* 44) "several lascivious passages" (47) connected with courtship and the wedding night were omitted that were in their source, a Latin poem "Asinarius." Similarly, Ernest Tonnelat (1912), likewise writing before the first publication of the 1810 manuscript, showed the Grimms at work as literary authors, and emphasized the care they—actually, Wilhelm—came to take as they saw the collection becoming a popular classic and children's book. Later, Kurt Schmidt, in a dissertation (1932), compared the versions in the manuscript of 1810 with the redactions of those tales in each of the seven editions of the complete collection, and also in the ten editions of the shorter anthology. Like Tonnelat, Schmidt pointed to Wilhelm's concern with the poetical qualities and appeal of the stories, noting the poetic embellishments and improvements introduced over the course of time.

Wilhelm Grimm's development of a particular style for fairy tales was studied subsequently by Wilhelm Schoof, who in a series of articles (1941, 1955, 1956/57, 1963) discussed stylistic and other changes made in four of the Grimms' tales: "Snow White" (*KHM* 53), "Fledgling" (*KHM* 51), "The Frog King" (*KHM* 1), and "Little Briar-Rose" (*KHM* 50). With regard to the latter tale, the Grimms' version of Sleeping Beauty, Schoof praised Wilhelm's gift for making the stories appealing for children while at the same time providing an artistic imitation of the style of folk narrative.

In connection with her attempt to show that Jacob and Wilhelm Grimm essentially agreed about style, form, and other matters in their literary editing and adapting of the stories from their sources, Gunhild Ginschel (1963) sought to characterize Jacob's style for fairy tales by analyzing his retelling of Basile's "The Serpent" (*Pentamerone*, II, 5)—which Jacob, with no mention of Basile, published (1816) in one of the then fashionable literary annuals called *Taschenbücher*. The Grimms went on to provide summary retellings of all fifty of Basile's tales in their volume of notes (1822) to the second edition of their collection. As Ginschel observed, the Grimms had possessed an edition of the *Pentamerone* since 1811 (Brentano, who likewise had an edition of it, had called that collection to their attention). The summaries of Basile's tales were dropped from the third edition of the notes (1856), because in the meantime, with the Grimms' encouragement, Felix Liebrecht had published a complete German translation of the *Pentamerone* (1846). Bolte and Polívka, however, made the Grimms' summaries of Basile's stories readily available again in their revised and much expanded edition of the Grimms' notes, referred to above (1913-32, see IV: 189-259). The literary qualities of the Grimms' renditions of the stories were stressed, too, by Alfred David and Mary Elizabeth David (1964). The Davids pointed to the Grimms' romanticism in changing or embellishing the stories to fit their notion of what folktales should be like ideally.

In addition to studying the changes in the stories made by the Grimms, scholars have investigated the identities of their sources, which the Grimms had concealed. In their copy of the first edition, however, they had noted down their informants for their own reference. As mentioned above, Wilhelm's son Herman Grimm (1897) used those notations to offer, for the first time, specific identification of the oral sources; and Herman then made the Grimms' copy of the first edition available to Johannes Bolte, who used the Grimms' notes and Herman's information to identify the informants for the users of his revised and expanded edition of the Grimms' notes to their collection.

An account of the Grimms' activities in collecting and publishing the two volumes of their first edition (1812 and 1815) was given by Wilhelm Schoof (1930), which he later revised and expanded (1959). In particular, Schoof provided information about the Grimms' informants and their relationships with those persons. Meanwhile, Richard Mehlem (1940) studied the Low German sources for the tales, especially as regards Lower Saxony.

As noted above, Heinz Rölleke made available highly reliable information on the Grimms' informants, beginning with his essay (1974a) about the sources for the Grimms' version of the Cinderella story (*KHM* 21) and for a less well known tale, "The Golden Bird" (*KHM* 57). Most importantly, Rölleke then demonstrated (1975) that the supposedly genuine Hessian tales by the servant woman "old Marie" were actually from a literarily interested young friend of Huguenot ancestry and background, Marie Hassenpflug. As Rölleke commented (82), "'Old Marie' now was a storyteller just so very much to the liking of many decidedly Hessian or German nationalist folktale researchers," whereas "precisely the contributions of Marie Hassenpflug display familiarity with the fairy-tale narratives of Perrault and Madame d'Aulnoy" (86). In Rölleke's edition (1975) of the 1810 manuscript, information on the sources is provided for each of the tales there (348-89) and about the individual informants (390-97); and in his edition (1980) of the Grimms' last edition of their collection (1857), he gives specific information on the Grimms' oral and literary sources for each title, as best known up to that time.

The identity of the Grimms' informants aside, there remains the question of the received versions' authenticity as folktale. Karl Schulte-Kemminghausen (1932, 18-19) raised the point that a source's telling of a tale in the presence of a transcriber, or collector of tales, represents a different situation from that of storytelling in the accustomed circle of listeners. The manner of a story's telling is inseparable from the conditions under which it is told. Even the Grimms' tales in Low German, which they did not stylistically alter in view of their relative lack of familiarity with the dialect, are as much artistic tales as folktale, all the more so considering that their informants, the aristocratic Haxthausen and Droste-Hülshoff families, displayed some reticence about retaining details that might offend against decorum. Rölleke made the point similarly in a recent essay (1986a, 107-08).

Regarding the authenticity of the Grimms' sources, there is also the question of the influence of literary versions on oral storytelling. Rolf Hagen, in his dissertation (1954), undertook a careful comparison of eight of Perrault's tales with the versions given by the Grimms. The direct and indirect literary influence was found to be considerable, but limited to some half-dozen of the Grimms' tales. Hagen also discussed the Grimms' borrowing of elements for these tales from other, German literary sources, especially those contemporaneous with the Grimms' first two editions (1812, 1815; 1819). In this way, Hagen shed further light on the literariness of the retellings in the Grimms' collection and the characteristic changes they made, especially in the direction of rendering the tales stories for children. In an essay published the following year (1955), Hagen argued that Perrault's tales did not seem to have become part of oral tradition in Germany by the Grimms' time. Instead, Perrault's influence on the *Children's and Household Tales* came either through literary sources or through Huguenot informants among their friends, like the Hassenpflugs.

The French Huguenot influence was further investigated by Ingeborg Weber-Kellermann (1970). She posed the question "Wherein lies the supposedly German character of the *Children's and Household Tales* if their origin demonstrably cannot be said to be exclusively German, as is generally assumed?" (432). Her answer was that the Grimms' success lay in their tailoring of the tales to the needs and tastes of the emerging burgher culture of their time, especially as regards the mothers' role in providing for their children the soon to be proverbial *gute Kinderstube*, or proper nursery upbringing.

Credit for helping disabuse the general reading public and the larger scholarly world of the notion that the *Kinder- und Hausmärchen* are folktales told exactly as they were in the Grimms' day in Germany belongs to the American Germanist John Ellis. In his book *One Fairy Story Too Many* (1983), he provocatively indicted the Grimms for literary fraud in their claiming to have published authentic popular tales collected from the common folk in Germany when they themselves knew better. Ellis extended his indictment, with some justification, to scholarship on the Grimms, stretching back to Tonnelat's study of 1912. Just as the Grimms had not been willing to confess the extent of the changes they had made and the Huguenot ancestry and culture of some of their informants, scholarly critics sometimes have resisted admitting that the Grimms were not being wholly open and honest with their readers about their sources and their handling of them.

Not only have scholars in recent years become ever more widely aware of the literariness of the Grimms' collection; there has also been increased concern with the question as to how we know of the existence of an oral tradition of folktale unaffected by literary sources. As Linda Dégh has commented (1988, 68-70),

> It is an irony that the documents from which folklorists infer the primacy of an oral tradition come from fixed literary and artistic versions. The themes can be traced back to literary documents of early simple narration, and there is little unanimity concerning when the oral genre *Märchen* emerged. [...] Critics who stated their belief in an oral tradition free from book influence, however, were not so far from the Grimmian principle in their own work. They did not record total storytelling events as social acts, as modern ethnographers do. We cannot speak of authenticity in our sense before the 1940s. The general public did not distinguish between oral narrator and tale writer and regarded published stories as common property free for anyone to change. Scholarly recording of oral tales from the folk, at the same time, meant notation of a skeleton content of stories judged to be genuine. [...] Small wonder that most published collections reflect the wishful thinking of folklorists, not the real folk repertoire: an oral tradition of miscellaneous provenience.

As Dégh observed, Albert Wesselski (1925; 1931) dated the emergence of fairy tale (*Märchen*) as a distinct genre from Straparola's *Nights* in the sixteenth century or even later with Basile and Perrault in the following century, and Rudolf Schenda (see Schenda, 1983, 28-30) "points out that the *Märchen*, earlier far less popular than jokes, horror, or personal experience accounts, became the literary fashion of high society only as late as the eighteenth century" (Dégh, 1988, 68).

In view of the vogue of literary fairy tales in France in the late seventeenth and the eighteenth century, one may ask whether this particular type of folktale existed in oral tradition in Germany independent of that fad. The craze for the literary use of magic and the marvelous in France during the reign of Louis XIV was the subject of an early study by P. Victor Delaporte (1891), followed several

decades later by Mary Elizabeth Storer's book (1928) focusing specifically on the vogue of *contes de fées* at the end of the seventeenth
century. The succeeding fashion of satirical and licentious fairy tales
in France in the eighteenth century was importantly investigated by
Jacques Barchilon, first in an essay on "Uses of the Fairy Tale in the
Eighteenth Century" (1963), then in his full-length study of that
subject (1975). Connections between the French literary vogue and
its subsequent rise in Germany were studied as early as Richard
Benz's 1906 dissertation. H. V. Velten (1930) offered a brief, not
especially enlightening essay on the influence of Perrault's tales on
German storytelling; and a comparative study of the Grimms' tales
and those of Perrault was done by Liliane Mourey (1978). Gonthier-
Louis Fink meanwhile (1966) provided a thorough study of that
vogue's importation into Germany in the half-century before the
beginning of the Grimms' activity in collecting folktales.

As we have seen, the issue whether fairy tales of the type found
in the Grimms' collection were being told in oral tradition in eighteenth-century Germany was recently raised by Manfred Grätz
(1988), whose thorough study on the question found no evidence of
such storytelling until shortly before the Grimms started their collection. Grätz's conclusion is that the genre arose in Germany only
gradually, in the second half of the eighteenth century, and under
the influence of French literary models. Regarding reports of the
storytelling in spinning rooms in Germany in that century, Grätz
maintains that "the majority of the testimonies indicate that as a
rule it was a matter of entertaining legends, superstitious ghost stories, and similar tales with a claim to truthfulness." (One may be
reminded here of Richard Wagner's nineteenth-century portrayal of
such storytelling in the spinning room in his opera *The Flying Dutch-
man*, where Senta's ballad mingles legend and ghost story.) Grätz's
finding on the basis of his extensive research was that "The express
mention, much less the writing down, of tales in the manner of the
Grimms' *Kinder- und Hausmärchen* does not occur in the eighteenth
century" (271).

The Grimms, indeed, in creating a new mode of tale, came to
reject the sort of horrifying stories that were part of earlier
storytelling. As Dieter Richter observed in an essay on the tale
"How Children Played Butcher," which the Grimms dropped after
the first edition, "precisely the stories that were eliminated [...] can
be illuminating for one who is interested in the complicated process
of the gradual development of the genre of Grimmian fairy tales"
(1986, 1).

When the Grimms' tales are viewed as literary products, not as
survivals of an ancient oral tradition, it no longer makes sense to
interpret them in connection with Germanic mythology in any narrower sense, such as had been done, for example, by Franz Linnig
in his late nineteenth-century book (1883) entitled "German Myth-

Fairy Tales: A Contribution to the Explanation of the Grimmian Children's and Household Tales." The same is then true for nationalistically motivated interpretations, such as Marie Luise Becker's finding (1901) that the Grimms' tales involving love display a specifically German ideal of the relationship between men and women, or Werner von Bülow's Wagneresque discussion of some of the Grimms' tales as runic fantasies related to a wildly fanciful Germanic mythology (1925, by a National Socialist press). Hermann Pongs's interpretation (1973) of a number of the Grimms' tales, while not explicitly nationalistic, extolled the simple folk beliefs and wisdom Pongs found contained in the stories.

Approaching the Grimms' tales as literature, indeed, weakens the case for ideological interpretations generally, to the extent that those interpretations presuppose the tales' descent from popular storytelling. The special importance assigned such stories by Jungian interpreters, like Joseph Campbell, Hedwig von Beit, and Marie-Louise von Franz, as broadly based manifestations of a collective unconscious is diminished. The Grimms' stories become ranged instead with other literary works that are studied by Jungian critics as reflecting the unconscious of particular individuals. The same holds true, of course, for Freudian criticism when the Grimms' tales are viewed as literary products. They become less the creations of a collective group, and need instead to be seen more in relation to the psychological make-up of particular individuals. The tales become emanations of the subconscious of specific persons. Bruno Bettelheim's Freudian study, seen in this light, needs to be understood as actually about "The Uses of Enchantment" by the various authors of the literary fairy tales he discusses.

There can be no question that Alan Dundes was justified recently in taking the psychoanalytic critics to task for assuming that the Grimms' tales and oral tradition were one and the same (1988, 18):

> Germanists and psychoanalysts [...] have had a long tradition of interpreting the Grimm tales. Since the founder and early practitioners of psychoanalysis were native speakers of German, it made sense for them to choose examples from the celebrated Grimm canon on those occasions when they sought to consider folklore as grist for the psychoanalytic mill. For one thing, it is never appropriate to analyze a folktale [...] on the basis of a single text. [...] The second problem from the folklorist's perspective is that the Grimms' versions of the tales are at least one step from pure oral tradition.

The problem raised though by Grätz's study, discussed above, is not only—as has long been recognized—that we cannot know just what pure oral tradition was like in the Grimms' time; there is reason to doubt that fairy tales in the narrower sense existed in oral tradition in Germany at all until shortly before the Grimms' collection and under the influence of French literary tales.

Beginning especially in the 1970s—in connection with increasing emphasis on historicity in literary studies, and above all in scholarship on German literature—there developed a corresponding swing toward approaching the Grimms' tales as literature. Jens Tismar, indeed, in his volume on literary fairy tales (1977) for the Metzler publishing house's series of handbooks, ranged the Grimms' stories among such *Kunstmärchen* as opposed to *Volksmärchen*, or 'folk fairy tales,' to which a separate volume in that series (Lüthi, 1962a) had been devoted. Similarly, Linda Dégh (1979) viewed the Grimms' collection as a popular literary classic in gauging the "social relevance" of its success since its first appearance.

The turn to the historical in literary study, which became evident in Germany around 1960, occurred at least partly in relation to, or response to, Marxist criticism. Among the studies in the 1970s that began to view the Grimms' tales specifically as literature, instead of folklore, was Jack Zipes's *Breaking the Magic Spell* (1979). Zipes, to be sure, saw the Grimm stories as deriving from oral tradition: "These *Märchen* were recorded during the first decade of the nineteenth century [...]. They were told in dialect, largely by servants, a watchman and inhabitants from towns and small cities and were stylized and transcribed into High German by the Grimms" (30). Yet Zipes wished to emphasize that the tales were products of that particular time and society: "a thorough analysis of the tales must take into account the background of the narrators and their communities, the social upheavals of the times caused by the Napoleonic Wars, the advent of mercantilism and the perspective of the Grimms, including their reasons for choosing certain tales for their collection" (30).

The leftward political direction reflected in Zipes's study was the product, too, of the various 'liberation' movements set in motion by the civil rights struggle that developed in the United States in the post-World War II period and reached a head in the 1960s. In literary studies, a major reflection of these liberation movements was the rise of feminist criticism in the 1970s and 1980s. Fairy tales, having often been thought to be literature by and for women ('old wives' tales'), became an early focus of study. At first, this interest was rather much in relation to the Walt Disney animated cartoons that, since their appearance beginning in the mid-1930s (*Snow White and the Seven Dwarfs*, 1937), had done so much to revive popular fascination with the genre. With reference to the Disney version of Snow White, and with Sleeping Beauty and other such romantic tales in mind, Marcia Lieberman (1972/73) and Kay Stone (1975) pointed to the passive female behavior idealized in such portrayals as reflecting a male-dominated, 'patriarchal' social order.

The feminist approach to folktales that sees in them an effort to use poetic art for purposes of subordinating the female gender is compatible with recent emphasis on folktale as literature instead of folklore. The more speculative feminist view of fairy tale that wishes to find its origins in prehistoric matriarchies, however, involves a return to Grimmian claims of the stories' ancient provenience. The chief example of this matriarchal approach is the book by Heide Göttner-Abendroth (1980).

As noted in our first chapter, the more moderate view that "the many fairy tales involving the wooing and winning of a princess [...] are remnants from [...] ancient belief in the powers of women" was expressed by Ruth Bottigheimer (1980, 12; see also 1982) the same year as the first appearance of Göttner-Abendroth's study. In Bottigheimer's series of publications on fairy tale beginning with that essay and culminating in her book *Grimms' Bad Girls & Bold Boys* (1987), she focused not on claims for the antiquity of the tales so much as on the Grimms' literary activity as editors, especially how their changes in the texts relate to feminist concerns. Still, she may be faulted for sometimes writing about the Grimms' rendition of a tale as though it had been substantially that way since antiquity, or even prehistoric times, or as though one has reliable evidence about how the tale was told then if it is indeed that old and can be presumed to be the same story. At other times, she assumes that from the Grimms' collection, or from surviving manuscripts, we know how a tale was narrated in their day. As Bottigheimer well recognizes, there may have been many tellers of the same tale and many differing versions.

Bottigheimer is on firmer ground when she confines her discussion to the significance of the changes the Grimms made between their manuscript of 1810, the first edition of 1812 and 1815, and the subsequent editions. Here she shows how, as editors and adapters, they—ultimately Wilhelm—tended increasingly to depict their female figures in ways that suited their pedagogical purposes and cultural aims. Moreover, Bottigheimer's book goes beyond feminist concerns to point to a wide range of elements in the Grimms' tales reflecting moral and social visions expressed through the stories (cf. the book's subtitle). And in a subsequent essay (1988), she reaches the interesting conclusion that changes made by the Grimms in succeeding editions reflect an increasing bourgeois idealization of folkways that brought with it a regressive model for the role of women.

A German feminist critic, Gertrud Jungblut, meanwhile had found the "model of the contemporary ideal of women," as conveyed in the Grimms' tales, to have been derived not from the folk but from "the infantilized doll-like women of nineteenth-century bourgeois society" (1986, 49). In reaching this quite opposite conclusion from Bottigheimer's, Jungblut's procedure was to compare the versions chosen by the Grimms with those they relegated to the notes (499):

If there were several versions of the same narrative material, the Grimms each time [as they wrote in their preface to the second edition of 1819] 'gave preference to the best one.' The best version was, in accord with their aims, the one most effective didactically. And in so far as we have to do with education, our point of departure must be that they had adopted the values of a patriarchal cultural tradition in which girls accordingly are pure, naive, innocent, stupid, docile, without a will of their own, passive, and in any case, however, *dependent* and *lacking in self-reliance* (Jungblut's emphasis).

Another German critic, Ingrid Spörk, focused her study (1985) not only on the younger women per se in the Grimms' tales, but on their relationship to the older women in the stories. Spörk's concern is with the mother-daughter relationship from a feminist perspective, though she employs terminology familiar from psychoanalytic criticism. She concludes (238) that the plot of the type of fairy tale she investigates is often set in motion by the lack or absence of a positive mother-figure, "the good nourishing mother" (238). Spörk argues, too, that the heroines' passivity, in the cases where this is so, may be explained as resulting from the "experience of a negative mother-imago or the mother as a negative person." The specifically feminist orientation of Spörk's argument lies in her suggestion that the patriarchal character of society explains the prevalence of these negative mother-figures, the severe punishment of them at the end of some stories, and the figure of the good fairy—as expressing the longing for a positive mother-figure.

Spörk, in reverting to the psychoanalytic approach, was not interested in the Grimms' role as revisers and adapters of the stories. Maria Tatar, however, while approaching the tales from a psychological viewpoint, took the Grimms' changes in their texts very much into consideration in her book *The Hard Facts of the Grimms' Fairy Tales* (1987). Somewhat like Bottigheimer (1987 and 1988), who showed that the Grimms tended increasingly to depict the roles of the sexes more as among the common folk than the upper classes, Tatar demonstrated that the Grimms inclined not only to retain, but also even to increase the role of violence and cruelty in the tales. As Tatar graphically put it, "Wilhelm Grimm may have found allusions to pregnancy offensive, but he had no such scruples about violence. He rarely let slip the opportunity to have someone burned at the stake, drowned, forced to dance in red-hot shoes, torn to pieces or stripped naked and put into a barrel studded with nails and harnessed to a horse" (181). Her point is not that this violence is gratuitous, but that the "victimization/retaliation pattern that appears in one tale after another [...] invites the depiction of heartless behavior and merciless punishment." Moreover, this pattern helps make the tales appealing to children, for the frequent "movement from victimization to retaliation gives vivid but disguised shape to the dreams of revenge that inevitably drift into the mind of every child beset by a sense of powerlessness" (190). Whereas Bottigheimer's feminist study approached the Grimms' tales as instilling in their young readers normative behavior linked to gender, Tatar's more psychological than social focus is on the stories' function of answering children's emotional needs.

The studies by Bottigheimer and Tatar were followed the next year by a book combining social and psychological approaches, Jack Zipes's volume of his collected essays entitled *The Brothers Grimm: From Enchanted Forests to the Modern World* (1988a). The subtitle of one of the essays can stand as a characterization of Zipes's focus of interest in all of the nine pieces brought together in the volume: "The Psycho-Social Origin of the Tales." Throughout, Zipes asks about the psychological motivations that explain the creation of the stories, especially the Grimms' adaptation of existing tales; and he places those motivations in a social context, particularly as understood in connection with the view of history as class struggle, including women's struggle for emancipation and liberation. On methodological grounds, Zipes may be criticized for sometimes claiming—as in his earlier book *Breaking the Magic Spell* (1979)— more than he can demonstrate, often arguing by assertion without citing the evidence, and occasionally pretending to know what cannot be known, for example, the nature and character of tales as they actually were transmitted at the time of the Grimms (much less how—if indeed—they were told before the Grimms' time).

My own contribution to discussion about the Grimms' tales as literature (McGlathery, *Fairy Tale Romance*, 1991) followed those by the other three American Germanists (Bottigheimer, Tatar, and Zipes). This study differed from theirs in focusing on only one type of story among the many in the Grimms' collection, the tales of love and marriage or *Liebesmärchen*. The aim was to investigate the depiction of typical roles and relationships in connection with stirrings of erotic passion. There are chapters, therefore, on brothers and sisters; on brides and their animal, or otherwise beastly, bridegrooms; on fathers and daughters; on older and younger women; on bold brides; and on less than bold suitors and bachelors. Unlike other studies approaching the Grimms' tales as literature, this one refrains from attempting to explain the nature and meaning of the changes the Grimms introduced into their texts, although in the notes attention is drawn to differing versions that were known to them (the version of the stories discussed in the main body of the study is that of the Grimms' last edition of 1857). At the same time, this study is comparative in that it investigates the similar roles and relationships depicted in the earlier collections of Basile and Perrault. The conclusion reached is that the erotic aspects of the typical roles and relationships tend to be readily apparent in Basile's early seventeenth-century Neapolitan tales, whereas they are not so obvious in Perrault's pieces done during the reign of Louis XIV and are still less visible in the Grimms' stories a hundred years thereafter in the Romantic period in Germany.

A large number of publications on the Grimms were occasioned by the bicentenary of their births in 1985-86, among them dozens on their *Kinder- und Hausmärchen*. A fair survey of the state of scholarly criticism on the Grimms' tales at that point is provided by the volume of essays *The Brothers Grimms and Folktale* (McGlathery, ed., 1988). The book resulted from one of the bicentennial commemorations, the international symposium held at the University of Illinois in April, 1986. Included are essays by 14 folklorists and Germanists from Germany and the United States. Five of the contributions had appeared earlier, and several more have been since re-published— in part or whole, unchanged or revised. The volume's virtue lay especially in its bringing together essays by prominent scholarly critics of the tales in one volume and all in English.

The Brothers Grimm and Folktale contains the following contributions:

Lutz Röhrich's argument (1984) that each version of a tale has its own meaning within a given cultural context;

Alan Dundes's interpretation of Little Red Riding Hood as depicting a "sequence of oral, anal, and finally genital themes" (43), in which he uses versions transmitted in broad, international oral tradition in preference to literary versions;

Kay Stone's return to her earlier subject of the Disney versions of fairy tales, this time to argue that even cinematic adaptation does not fix the 'text' of a tale once and for all and for all viewers, anymore than did the Grimms' telling of Snow White;

Linda Dégh's defense of the Grimms to folklorists as having provided future tellers of folktale with material for adapting, and adding to, their repertoires;

Donald Ward's rebuttal to John Ellis's indictment of the Grimms (1983) for having committed literary fraud in passing off their stories as authentic folktale;

Heinz Rölleke's demand (1986a) that scholarly critics begin with the version of a given tale in the Grimms' last edition and proceed backwards in time, trying "to uncover one layer of the text's development after the other" (108);

Wolfgang Mieder's analysis of exactly how and why Wilhelm Grimm, as he reported in the preface to the sixth edition (1850), was "Ever Eager to Incorporate Folk Proverbs"—a subject to which a volume of essays edited by Heinz Rölleke that same year (1988) was also devoted;

Maria Tatar's contention that the Bluebeard story (the Grimms eliminated their version between the first and second editions) was originally about "the heroine's quite legitimate *cognitive* curiosity" (135, Tatar's emphasis) before the morals appended to the story by Perrault made it a tale cautioning against female curiosity;

Gonthier-Louis Fink's demonstration of particularly convincing lower-class perspectives in the tales the Grimms had from an old soldier;

August Nitschke's study of accounts of storytelling in the several centuries leading up to the Grimms for hints about the evolution of that activity's meaning and function;

Walter Scherf's similar investigation of the role storytelling played in the Grimms' lives in the early years of their collecting of tales;

Ruth Bottigheimer's discussion of how, from the refined, or bourgeois, nature of the tales that characterized the 1812 volume, there followed a trend, beginning with the second volume in 1815, to coarser material, of a type to be associated rather with the folk, so that the depiction of women and their treatment became increasingly misogynous and harsh;

Jack Zipes's probing of how psychosocial elements influenced the Grimms' relationship to their activity of collecting and publishing folktales;

Betsy Hearne's essay on how economic shifts in juvenile publishing have resulted in the Grimms' texts being modified in the competition for broader markets.

Much of the philological basis for current study of the Grimms' *Kinder- und Hausmärchen* has been provided by Heinz Rölleke, Professor of German at the University of Wuppertal in Germany. Over the course of the 1970s and 1980s, Rölleke has established himself as the leading authority on the literary culture that surrounded and shaped the Grimms' collection. His work in this area has been characterized by careful sifting of documentary evidence—published and unpublished—and by judicious review of previously held assumptions about the stories' provenience and the Grimms' practice in editing and collecting them.

In addition to his numerous publications on individual tales and other particular matters, Rölleke's editorial work on the Grimms' collection has made scholarly study of the tales as literature easier. The first in this series of editions was the extremely useful and influential volume (1975) discussed earlier that made available a reliable text of the 1810 manuscript juxtaposed with the versions of those stories in the succeeding first edition of 1812. Five years later (1980), Rölleke edited, for the Reclam paperback series, the Grimms' seventh and last edition of their full collection (1857), including the third edition (1856) of their volume of notes to the tales, as well as the 28 stories that had formed a part of the collection at one point or another but had been eliminated by the time of the Grimms' last edition. Rölleke's handy Reclam edition also provides his own commentary on the transmission of the individual stories and the changes made over the course of the seven editions done by the Grimms, together with bibliographical references to the relevant secondary literature (he expressly excluded, however, reference to interpretive studies). Rölleke also offered tables showing the publication dates for each of the tales through the eight editions and indicating the story's transmitters or sources, to the extent this was known. There is a useful bibliography, and a judicious and informative afterword. In this way, Rölleke assembled something modestly approaching a—yet to be undertaken—scholarly edition of the Grimms' collection; and he did so in a pocketbook format priced well within the reach of students and the general reading public.

Many of the Grimms' more important changes in the collection were made between the first edition of 1812 and 1815 and the second edition. To help facilitate study of those changes, Rölleke edited a reprint of that edition of 1819 (1982). Meanwhile, three editions of his selection of texts from the Grimms' posthumous papers were published (1977; 3rd ed. 1983). This was a sample of stories the Grimms had among their manuscripts but chose not to include. The material was by and large not unknown to scholars; much or most of it indeed had been published in various places. The volume's importance lay in making some four-dozen such texts readily available. Rölleke's aim with this publication was "to convey an impression about the sort of material from which the Grimms created their [...] editions of fairy tales and legends" (4). That aim was fulfilled especially in the negative sense that one sees that the Grimms made the right choice in excluding these texts.

Rölleke followed these editions with a facsimile one (1986) of the Grimms' own copy of the first edition (1812, 1815) of the *Kinder- und Hausmärchen*. This publication served both to make that original edition itself more readily available and, most importantly, also to place before one's eyes (and with decipherment provided) the Grimms' notations made in the margins. Scholars no longer had to visit the Grimm Museum in Cassel to study these notations. The Grimms' annotations are of importance in themselves, but have added significance when checked against the changes made in the second edition and the notes to that edition. Which changes, comment, or observations found their way into subsequent editions, and which did not, and if not, why not? To facilitate such comparisons, Rölleke provided a synopsis of the numbering of the tales in the first and second editions. He also outlined some of the conclusions that can be drawn, from the Grimms' marginal notations, about the dates on which they heard or received the tales from the contributors. Also, since Jacob's and Wilhelm's handwriting can be distinguished, their copy with their notations sheds light on their respective roles in working on the collection between the first and second editions.

That same year, Rölleke published an essay in which he summarized new results of research on the Grimms' collection. There he outlined how a proper study of that work, as literature, needed to be conducted (1986a, 101-02):

> [...] a serious and comprehensive philological investigation of *Grimms' Fairy Tales* would have to consist of some 240 individual studies, since that many texts play a part in the printing history and success of this work. There were 211 texts in the edition of 1857, the last during the Grimms' lifetime, and thirty texts that were eliminated along the way in the course of the previous editions, not to mention numerous parallel versions about which the Grimms reported in their scholarly commentary on the stories. For each text, one would need to describe its history before the Grimms; to uncover the form in which the Grimms became familiar with the tale, through hearing or reading it; and to document and interpret the changes made, whether as a result of a misunderstanding, for reasons of stylistic improvement, motivation, embellishment, or abridgement, or above all as the result of manifold contamination. And this must be done not only for the first edition of 1812-15, but for all seventeen editions of the collection (seven of the full version, and ten of the short version), taking into account, of course, the manuscript material in the form of inscribed notations and textual changes.

We shall want to keep Rölleke's philological admonitions in mind as we turn finally to scholarly criticism on individual stories, types of tale, and particular motifs.

3. Individual Stories and Motifs

A. Identifying Types of Tales

THE GEOGRAPHICAL-HISTORICAL, OR 'FINNISH,' approach to folktale that flourished in the early twentieth century focused attention on similarities among stories. Assigning tales to categories called 'types' was a means to the end of determining the geographical distribution of that story's occurrence and the history of its dissemination. This aim was not unrelated to nationalistic desires to claim a part of oral tradition for one's own country, as the Grimms had done in asserting that shared European folktale traditions originated with the Germanic peoples. In the main, however, the Finnish school, being a group of scholars from various nations, was characterized by an internationalist spirit which, like the Grimms' Enlightenment predecessor Johann Gottfried Herder with his collection of folksongs from different countries, aimed at an appreciation of each people's contributions, as reflecting its particular culture.

Identifying types of stories was important, too, for the succeeding formalistic approach to folktale that arose in the 1920s. Here the aim was rather to define folktale as a genre, especially for purposes of distinguishing fairy tale from legend and other "simple" forms of popular narrative, as Jolles (1930) had called them. Like the issue of the tales' origins and dissemination, the question of genre had been posed by the Grimms, especially the distinction between fairy tale (*Märchen*) and legend (*Sage*). The Grimms had been concerned with distinguishing genres in connection with their claim for the timelessness, or timeless setting and perspective, of fairy tale—the genre's quality of immortality in that sense. The formalistic approach, though, was a distinctly philological or literary one, relatively divorced from political and cultural ideology.

Recognition of the role of identifiable story types, and especially the existence of common motifs, has important implications as well for the study of the Grimms' tales as literature. The Grimms' recognition of, and familiarity with, recurring types and common motifs as being characteristic of folktale demonstrably played a role in their shaping of their stories. Moreover, beyond the question of changes the Grimms made in their stories is how each change of a motif, or in a motif, affects the meaning of the tale. Most important of all, how do the functions of motifs vary from story to story with regard to the question of meaning?

Among early studies identifying characteristics of the genre of fairy tale, or of certain story types, was Robert Petsch's on formulaic endings (1900). In his 1922 dissertation, Adolf Genzel viewed the role of helpers and adversaries as the chief formative principle in fairy tale, while Martti Haavio (1929) and Albert Wesselski (1933) wrote about the type of the "chain tale," in which one action leads to the next in uncanny succession, as happens, for example, in the Grimms' stories "The Louse and the Flea" (*KHM* 30) and "Herr Korbes" (*KHM* 41). Max Lüthi's doctoral thesis (1943) was on the role of gifts in fairy tale and legend.

The appearance of animals in fairy tales has been cited as a particular characteristic. The part played by animals endowed with souls was discussed by Hildegard Hendricks (1951), who took up each genus and species individually. Lutz Röhrich (1953) discussed the relationship between animals and humans, especially the animals' role as helpers or as bridegrooms. J. Mendelsohn wrote about animal fairy tales from a psychological viewpoint, "as an Expression of the Structure of Psychic Development" (1961). The motif of the grateful dead, meanwhile, had been commented upon by Johannes Bolte (1915).

Types of stories, as opposed to individual motifs, have been the subject of a number of studies. An early example was that by P. Arfet on the type of the "substituted bride" (1897). Examples of the type of the dragon-slayer were discussed by Wilhelm Wisser (1925). Kurt Ranke (1934) investigated the tale of two brothers, like the Grimms' story of that name (*KHM* 60). Marianne Rumpf set out to trace the origin of cautionary tales (1955). The role of oldest and youngest siblings was discussed by Marianne Handschin-Ninck (1956), and Warren Roberts wrote on the stories about "Kind and Unkind Girls" (1958). Heino Gehrts (1967) studied tales about brothers in European folktale, seeing the motif of a brother's sacrifice for his brother as a survival from classical antiquity.

In addition to the stories about brothers, depiction of other family relationships has been found characteristic of fairy tale as well. Drawing on earlier anthropological studies like those of James Frazer (1890), Alfred Winterstein (1928) focused, from a psychoanalytic perspective, on depictions of daughters' passage to womanhood in fairy tale as originating in primitive puberty rites, noting that in these tales the daughter is often cast out, secluded, put in a tower or in the care of an older woman, protected from some unseen danger, or instructed in the domestic arts. Bruno Jöckel (1939), likewise from a psychoanalytic viewpoint, emphasized the importance of relationships between daughters and the other men in the family: "In our view, the brother is for the sister, and the father for the daughter, [...] the representative of the male principle, toward which the girl first has to have assumed a clear, affirmative position before she goes about choosing *the* man with whom she wants to share her life" (62, Jöckel's emphasis). Günther Bittner (1963) took a similarly Freudian view of the sister's emotional and developmental position between her father and her brothers.

Mothers and maternal figures in fairy tale have likewise been an object of study. Wilhelm Laiblin (1936) applied Jungian theory to this subject. Sibylle Birkhäuser-Oeri (1976), too, interpreted mother and daughter relationships from a Jungian viewpoint. Recent commentary, though, has been mostly from a decidedly feminist perspective. In an early example, Marthe Robert, discussing the role of older women, maintained that "Although her characteristics have been considerably downgraded, the old woman in Grimms' tales has partially retained her role as guardian of rites and tradition" (1967, 49). Commenting on the frequent role of stepmothers, Karen Rowe observed that the stepdaughter's "maturation signals [the stepmother's] own waning sexual attractiveness and control [...] both in life and in fairy tale, time triumphs, delivering the daughter to inescapable womanhood and the stepmother to aged oblivion and death" (1979, 241).

These conclusions about older women in their role vis-à-vis the heroines of fairy tale point to the importance of erotic desire in many stories. As Marthe Robert noted, if the older woman's function originally concerned mating rituals, "one at least can understand the paradox of the tale which, at all times intended for children, gives preferential treatment to the subject the least appropriate to children's literature: the erotic quest of the beloved through a thousand painful trials" (1967, 50). Much earlier, Walter Berendsohn had raised that same point: "If fairy tale is to serve as children's literature it has to be slightly reshaped, since love after all guides and directs everything [...]. The natural, sexual things are to be sure not particularly emphasized, but also are not circumvented" (1921, 37). I reached the same conclusion, too, in my study about love and marriage in fairy tale (McGlathery, 1991).

The type of tale popularly familiar from Jeanne-Marie Leprince de Beaumont's "Beauty and the Beast" ("La Belle et la Bête," 1756) has attracted quite special attention. Mme Leprince de Beaumont used the motif of the animal suitor to create a morally edifying, thoroughly literary story with a pedagogical aim: the inculcation of an ideal of goodness and loving kindness in young girls, for whom her *Magasin des Enfants*, in which the tale appeared, was intended. Among folklorists and scholars, however, this type of story has been viewed especially in connection with Apuleius's tale of "Cupid and Psyche" in his *The Golden Ass*, from the second century A.D. Ernst Tegethoff's dissertation (1922) was devoted to the Amor and Psyche

type, as depicting a union with a magical spouse (a "Martenehe").
Elisabeth Koechlin subsequently sought to identify distinguishing
features of the Amor and Psyche and animal groom types (1945).
And Jan-Öjvind Swahn (1955) produced a full-scale folkloristic
monograph on the type of the supernatural husband, including the
animal bridegroom.

More recently, the type of the animal groom has been approached interpretively. Max Lüthi judged that the motif "originally
had erotic meaning" (Lüthi, 1947, 66). Erich Neumann (1952) sub-
jected Apuleius's story to a Jungian interpretation. Bruno Bettelheim
found the motif's meaning to be the overcoming of "a negative attitude toward sex." These stories "simply teach that for love, a radical change in previously held attitudes about sex is absolutely necessary. What must happen is expressed, as always in fairy tales,
through a most impressive image: a beast is turned into a magnifi-
cent person" (1976, 282). Regarding Mme Leprince de Beaumont's
literary tale, Bettelheim saw evidence of "Beauty's oedipal attachment to her father not only by her asking him for a rose, but also by
our being told in detail how her sisters went out enjoying themselves at parties and having lovers while Beauty always stayed
home and told those who courted her that she was too young to
marry and wanted 'to stay with her father a few years longer'"
(307). Concerning the animal groom type in general, Karen Rowe
similarly commented, "Many tales implicitly acknowledge the po-
tent attraction between females and the father; but as purveyors of
cultural norms, they [i.e., the tales] often mask latent incest as filial
love and displace blatant sexual desires onto a substitute, such as a
beast [...]" (1979, 243-44).

Maria Tatar, however, found "the deeper significance of these
metamorphoses" to be that "the heroine sees in her husband-to-be
nothing but the incarnation of bestial impulses" (1987, 171). Tatar
went on to note, though, that "it is generally the human bridegrooms who indulge in shockingly uncivilized behavior [...]. Their
bestial counterparts, by contrast, are models of decorum and dig-
nity." In a subsequent essay, Tatar formulated the distinction between the two types of grooms in the Grimms' tales this way: "First,
there are the animal grooms who make life unpleasant for many a
female protagonist: these are the frogs, bears, hedgehogs, and other
creatures who press themselves on attractive young girls. But these
beasts invariably turn out to be handsome young princes in disguise
and generally prove to be perfect gentlemen. The real fairy-tale
beasts, even if they are beasts only in the figurative rather than the
literal sense of the term, turn out to be murderers masquerading as
civilized men" (1988, 133). My judgment, similar to that of the
Freudian critics who view the stories as depicting a process of
maturation, was that the animal suitor and beastly bridegroom types

"portray crises related to thoughts of marrying or the wedding night" on the part of these nubile maidens (McGlathery, 1991, 55).

While it is important, in discussing the Grimms' tales as literature, to recognize the types to which the given story belongs, and which folktale motifs it employs, we do well to take Heinz Rölleke's advice, quoted at the end of the preceding chapter, that each tale must be studied in its own right. Accordingly, we turn our attention now to critical commentary on the individual tales, beginning with some of those that are better known in the United States.

B. Ten Best-Known Tales

The Frog Prince

Chosen by the Grimms to lead off their collection, this story (*KHM* 1) is an example of the animal groom type we have just been discussing. As such, it has attracted special attention from Freudian critics. Bruno Jöckel concluded that "In this 'king's daughter' we may see a girl who is about to cross the boundary between childhood and maturity" (1948, 205). Bruno Bettelheim observed, "The closer the frog comes to the girl physically, the more disgusted and anxious she gets, particularly about being touched by it. The awakening of sex is not free of disgust or anxiety [...]" (1976, 288). As Jack Zipes then noted, in the version the Grimms had in their manuscript of 1810, "the frog has no other desire than to sleep with [the girl]" and the tale "is explicitly sexual" (1983a, 50). Lutz Röhrich similarly concluded that "without a doubt, in the case of the 'Frog King' we are dealing, at bottom, with a decidedly erotic tale, not with a story for children" (1986b, 20). I subsequently pointed out that, as the Grimms told the story in the first edition (1812), the princess does not hesitate for a moment to join the 'frog' in her bed, now that he is lying there as a prince; moreover, in the 1810 version the transformation clearly happens only when the prince has survived the princess's hurling him against the wall by bouncing off onto her mattress, suggesting that the 'magical' requirement for reversing the 'evil' transformation was that he succeed in getting into her bed (1991, 59). Other criticism on this story has included Wilhelm Schoof's use of it (1956/57) to exemplify types of changes the Grimms made as they developed their own fairy-tale style, and Lutz Röhrich's account (1979) of parodies of the story, including those in cartoons.

Tale of One Who Went Off to Learn Fear

This story (*KHM* 4) itself is not well known in the United States, but its main motif is familiar to opera-goers from Richard Wagner's appropriation of it in *The Ring of the Nibelung* for the characterization of his young hero Siegfried. Wagner's Siegfried learns fear through encountering the slumbering Brünnhilde after he has arrived at sexual maturity without having ever laid eyes on a woman (*Siegfried*, act III, sc. 3).

Such use of the motif for conveying erotic meaning has of course especially interested Freudian critics. Bruno Jöckel offered the following interpretation of the concluding episode of the Grimms' tale, in which the bridegroom is doused by his bride and her chambermaid with a bucket of fish to cure him of his preoccupation with learning how it feels to have goose flesh: "When he then feels the fish, emblematic of male procreation, and the water, symbol of the female, pressing in upon him, the spell is finally broken. Now he knows what getting the creeps is" (1939, 76). Still more speculative was Zillinger's interpretation of the whole tale as a symbolic representation of the process of maturation—which Wagner in his opera perhaps did indeed make of it. Especially bold was Zillinger's claim that the first night the youth spends in the haunted castle symbolically depicts masturbatory urges, as "the first entirely animalistic-carnal sexual stirrings and the overcoming of them" (1963, 112). Zillinger defined the maturation involved in a non-erotic way, however, as "a path from dependency to self-responsibility, from inauthenticity to authenticity" (107), echoing themes familiar from the existentialist philosophy dominant in the post-World War II period in the West.

Like Zillinger, Carl-Heinz Mallet (1965) understood the tale to be a symbolic representation of developmental processes in puberty, particularly autoeroticism and masturbation as a stage leading toward sexual maturity, the latter defined as achievement of the capacity to love. Bruno Bettelheim's conclusion was that "it was sexual anxiety that led to the hero's inability to shudder [...]. Because it is a fear of which only his wife is able to cure him at night in bed, this is a sufficient hint of the underlying nature of the anxiety" (1976, 281). Heinz Rölleke, by contrast, interpreted learning to know fear as learning to fear death (1979). My own judgment was similar to Bettelheim's, but I interpreted the youth's obsession as a regressive preoccupation that "renders his newlywed wife dissatisfied with him as a lover" (McGlathery, 1991, 157), hence her desire to cure him of that compulsion. In an early study on this tale, Wilhelm Wisser (1924) attempted to reconstruct the main outlines of the story in the form he assumed it must have had when originally invented, before changes occurred in the course of its oral transmission.

Rapunzel
Concerning this story (*KHM* 12) of a girl locked away in a tower by a jealous witch, Ernest Tonnelat noted that while in the Grimms' first edition (1812) Rapunzel's having had intercourse with the prince (whom she has hauled up into the tower with her hair)

comes to light when she complains to the witch that "my little clothes are getting so tight and don't want to fit me anymore," in the second edition (1819) this reference to pregnancy was suppressed. Rapunzel's talk about her clothes no longer fitting was replaced by her question to the witch about why it is harder to pull her up into the tower than the prince. Tonnelat observed (1912, 98-99) that this change still did not render the tale proper as children's literature because, while Rapunzel may not know what the consequences of sexual relations can be, by this time she obviously has been engaging in premarital intercourse with her prince.

Max Lüthi identified the Grimms' immediate source for their "Rapunzel" as a German translation of the French version entitled "Persinette" by Mlle de la Force (Charlotte-Rose de Caumont de la Force), a contemporary of Charles Perrault. Lüthi applauded the Grimms' changing of the heroine's name from "Petersilchen" (Little Parsley) in the German source, but observed that "In folk belief the plants named Rapunzel play no important role," while eroticizing powers were ascribed to parsley (1959, 79; see also 1958).

The imprisoning of Rapunzel in the tower has been of particular interest to feminist critics. Kay Stone commented, "We must look closely to discover that it is at puberty that Rapunzel is locked in a tower, Snow White is sent out to be murdered, and Sleeping Beauty is put to sleep [...] this restriction of women at puberty can also be interpreted as a reaction of men to the threat of female sexuality" (1975, 46-47). My view was that the story is about an older woman's efforts "to prevent the fulfillment of young desire" out of jealous attachment to the girl (McGlathery, 1991, 120).

Hansel and Gretel

Heinz Rölleke has shown (1983b) that, in its ultimate form, the Grimms' version of this story (*KHM* 15), together with that of "The Wolf and the Seven Young Kids" (*KHM* 5), was influenced by another literary collection of tales, the *Elsässische Volksmärchen* of August Stöber (1842). Among earlier interpretive comment on this story was Bruno Jöckel's identification of the witch as "the second embodiment of the stepmother" : "therefore we are not surprised that after Gretel has killed the witch, the children find that the stepmother meanwhile has died as well" (1939, 127). The significance of changes made by the Grimms between the first edition (1812) and the last (1857) were studied by Elisabeth Winter (1962). Hans Traxler published (1963) an elaborate spoof on folkloristic studies in which he purported to document "the truth" about Hansel and Gretel, showing that the story had a basis in history in view of archeological and other evidence. Helmut Brackert (1980) selected the story to demonstrate problems of interpreting fairy tales. I concluded that the focus of the tale is on innocent devotion between siblings of opposite sex (McGlathery, 1991, 27-29).

Cinderella

This tale (*KHM* 21) was among the first for which a thorough geographical-historical survey was undertaken, that by Marian Roalfe Cox (1892), which listed, and gave summaries of, the variants of this story type known up to that time. Cox included stories of the "Thousandfurs" type (*KHM* 65) as well, and also tales involving the motif—familiar from Shakespeare's *King Lear*—of the youngest daughter cast out by her father because he misunderstands her response to his demand that she tell him how much she loves him (as happens, too, in the Grimms' "The Goosegirl at the Spring," *KHM* 179). The same sort of study on the Cinderella type was undertaken a second time as well in a dissertation by Anna Birgitta Rooth (1951).

Interpretive commentary on the Cinderella story has focused on various motifs. Hermann Bausinger (1955) judged the shoe to symbolize the heroine's beauty, small feet being an indication of that attribute. Beryl Sandford (1967) discussed Cinderella in relation to his clinical practice of psychoanalysis. Bruno Bettelheim, from a Freudian viewpoint, focused on Cinderella's relationship to her widower father and her stepmother: "If Cinderella is to become master of her own fate, her parents' authority must be diminished. The diminution and transfer of power could be symbolized by the branch knocking the father's hat off his head, and also the fact that the same branch grows into a tree that has magical powers for Cinderella. Therefore, that which diminished the father (the branch of the hazel tree) is used by Cinderella to increase the power and prestige of the archaic (dead) mother" (1976, 257).

Perrault's version of the tale was approached by Timothy Murray (1976) from the standpoint of the anthropological theories of Claude Lévi-Strauss, and was used by Joseph Courtès (1976) to exemplify a semiotic approach to literature. Employing an "historical-behavioral" method, August Nitschke (1980) studied the Cinderella story as a source of information about earlier periods, including prehistoric times. Kay Stone's comments addressed the feminist concern regarding the message of romantic fairy tales "for modern girls and women." She found that message to be "the rewards one is supposed to receive for being pretty, polite, and passive; the primary reward, of course, is marriage, and marriage not just to anyone but to a 'prince,' someone who can provide status and the benefits of a beautiful life" (1985, 136-37). Like Bettelheim's, my focus was on the heroine's relationship to her father and her deceased mother, but less in the context of psychoanalytic theory than in comparison with similar portrayals in Basile's and Perrault's versions of the story type (McGlathery, 1991, 98, 108, 117-18). An anthology of commentary on the Cinderella tale, with a critical bibliography, was provided by Alan Dundes (1982).

Little Red Riding Hood

The story that has attracted the most critical commentary is surely this tale (*KHM* 26). Paul Delarue published a folkloristic study of this story type (1950/51), in which he argued that Charles Perrault's source for his famous literary version was oral tradition, namely stories like the versions seemingly independent of Perrault's tale that had been collected from oral sources since the mid-nineteenth century. Delarue contended that Perrault adapted such a version in accord with the tastes of his time and audience, notably through avoiding crudities and improprieties in the oral versions, like the girl's eating of her grandmother's flesh and blood, at the wolf's invitation, and her escape from the wolf by claiming that she must go relieve herself. Delarue contended, too, that interpretations of the story as being symbolic must pay attention to the features of the oral as well as the written versions. In particular, he maintained that the red hood was an accessory not necessarily belonging to versions before Perrault, since it was not always found in oral tradition.

That same year, Marianne Rumpf (1951) likewise undertook, in her dissertation, a geographical-historical study of the Red Riding Hood tale. In her subsequent essay on tales of terror and warning (1955), Rumpf put forth the thesis that Red Riding Hood's adversary was originally a werewolf, which she argued seemed "the more probable as soon as one is able to look into the court records according to which, in French cities in the sixteenth and seventeenth centuries, men presumed to be werewolves were accused and convicted" (1955, 5). She found in some court records that these supposed werewolves, considered male counterparts of witches as ogresses, appear to have been attracted by the color red.

Unlike Delarue and Rumpf, most interpreters of Little Red Riding Hood have based their comments on the literary versions of the Grimms or Perrault. Erich Fromm found the Grimms' version to depict male-female conflict (1951, 235). Fromm claimed the girl's red cap is "a symbol of menstruating," and that therefore "The little girl of whose adventures we hear has become a mature woman and is now confronted with the problem of sex" (240). When the girl is warned by her mother not to stray from the path so that she will not fall and break the bottle, the warning secretly concerns "the danger of sex and of losing her virginity." Fromm judged the tale was told from a woman's point of view and is "an expression of deep antagonism against men and sex" (241). Since, in the Grimms' version, the wolf is killed and the girl and her grandmother are rescued from its stomach, the tale is "a story of triumph by man-hating women." All in all, "The male is portrayed as a ruthless and cunning animal, and the sexual act is described as a cannibalistic act in which the male devours the female" (240).

Felix Freudmann (1963) judged Perrault's statements of the tale's moral to be incongruous when compared with the action in the story; the lessons Perrault appended were expressions of his realism in the face of all the magic found in folktale. Lilla Veszy-Wagner's Freudian commentary (1966) was in relation to her clinical experience of patients' dreams and fantasies involving the Red Riding Hood story. The following year, Jacques Barchilon discussed Perrault's relating of the marvelous to the realistic in this story and others, with particular reference to Perrault's handling of erotic matters (1967). That same year, Lutz Röhrich's essay on modern parodies of Red Riding Hood appeared (1967). Marc Soriano, the following year, analyzed Perrault's text as a literary adaptation, in part with reference to Delarue's observations earlier (1950/51) about oral versions, since collected, that do not seem influenced by Perrault. In view of these oral versions, the girl's red cap or hood as such, including its significance as a gift from grandmother, is not an essential feature of the story as a type, Soriano concluded (1968b).

Expression of various views on Red Riding Hood continued in the 1970s. In a novelistic, almost word-by-word commentary on Perrault's text, Georges Londeix viewed it as a story of seduction that Perrault might just possibly have invented (1970). Lee Burns (1972) approached the tale as children's literature, in which innocent eroticism is involved on the little girl's part (wanting to cuddle up with grandmother), while the wolf's mind is on seduction. Correspondingly, the child reader responds to the—erotically tinged—element of fear, while the adult reader senses the eroticism more directly. Burns also compared Perrault's text with the Grimms' version, with some more recent ones, and with the oral French versions in which the girl escapes from the wolf by going outside to relieve herself, the innocent eroticism here being scatological. Burns's approach focused on erotic implications in the story without invoking Freudian theory as such.

While Burns's essay reflected the trend in literary criticism toward considering how readers may react to literature ('reception theory'), Hans-Wolf Jäger's comparison of the Grimms' version with their Romantic contemporary Ludwig Tieck's earlier adaptation of the story as a fairy-tale play (*Märchendrama*) belonged to another critical approach gaining favor in the 1970s, the relation between literature and politics. Jäger (1974) argued that Tieck, in his play *Rotkäppchen*, had established a degree of symbolic association between the girl's red cap and the cap of that color worn by the Jacobins in the French Revolution, between the wolf and the partisans of the Revolution as rebels and outsiders championing liberty, and between the hunter and the servants of monarchical tyranny. Moreover, Jäger maintained, the Grimms, in borrowing some elements of their tale from Tieck's play, would not have been unaware of these symbolic political associations. (Jäger's last name, meaning 'hunter,' and his first name, containing 'wolf,' may not have been unrelated to his interest in the story, especially the Tieck and Grimm versions, in which there is a hunter as well as a wolf.)

The 1970s also saw the rise of semiotics as a critical method, which Victor Laruccia applied in an essay on Red Riding Hood (1975). Laruccia's—frightfully abstract—analysis of Perrault's text was based particularly on the anthropological and structuralist theories of Claude Lévi-Strauss, as well as on communication theory. By far the most widely heard critical voice on the tales in the 1970s, however, belonged to Bruno Bettelheim. Especially intriguing was Bettelheim's focus, from a Freudian viewpoint, on the grandmother's gift of the red hood or cap to the granddaughter: "Whether it is Mother or Grandmother—this mother once re-moved—it is fatal for the young girl if this older woman abdicates her own attractiveness to males and transfers it to the daughter by giving her a too attractive red cloak [...]. Red is the color symboliz-ing violent emotions, very much including sexual ones" (1976, 173). A cautionary message was found, too, by Carole Hanks and D. T. Hanks, in their essay two years later, but it was a philosophical, not a psychological message. They judged that Perrault's tale, in con-trast to the Grimms' version with its 'double' happy ending, "points out that maturity is risky; there *are* dangers in the forest—if the maturing person makes a misstep (not necessarily through any per-sonal fault), then he or she may perish" (1978, 95; the Hankses' emphasis).

By the arrival of the 1980s, the body of criticism on Red Riding Hood had grown large enough that attention now centered on re-viewing and evaluating such commentary, including the many parodies and adaptations of the tale done over the years. In this shift we may see reflected a growing trend toward 'historicity' in critical studies—a 'Geschichtlichkeit' that has included the history of academic disciplines, or *Wissenschaftsgeschichte*.

The first such investigation regarding Red Riding Hood was that by Hans Ritz, a paperback (1981) addressed to a general readership that appeared in a tenth, revised edition in 1992. The value of Ritz's little book lay especially in its critical survey of commentary on the story by others. Though he does not venture an interpretation of his own, he does offer the opinion that the story's message is "the world is not worthy of the trust we originally bring to it" (130).

Ritz's presentation was followed by Jack Zipes's *Trials and Tribu-lations of Little Red Riding Hood* (1983b). The subtitle, "Versions of the Tale in a Sociocultural Context," reflects Zipes's aim to demonstrate how adaptations of this story express aims and values of the soci-eties and groups in which they arise. Assuming that oral versions of Red Riding Hood, even though they have been collected only since the nineteenth century, represent the story as originally told, Zipes emphasized that "In the folk tale the little girl displays a natural, relaxed attitude toward her body and sex and meets the challenge of the would-be seducer," whereas in Perrault's literary version the girl "is chastised because she is innocently disposed toward nature in the form of the wolf and the woods, and she is *raped* or punished because she is guilty of not controlling her natural inclinations" (29; Zipes's emphasis).

Following the books by Ritz and Zipes, the third such study of criticism, parodies, and adaptations of this story was Alan Dundes's *Little Red Riding Hood: A Casebook* (1989), with a critical bibliography of interpretations and other commentary on the tale (239–47). In an essay on "Interpreting Little Red Riding Hood Psychoanalytically" (1988), reprinted in his "Casebook," Dundes, preferring certain versions told internationally in oral tradition to the literary versions of the Grimms and Perrault, judged that "the evidence of the infantile nature of LRRH has been available for centuries, but folklorists and literary scholars have chosen not to consider such evidence. The oral cannibalistic eating of the mother's [i.e., the grandmother's] body, the reference to defecating in bed, the toddler's rope [...], and for that matter the very insistence upon Red Riding Hood's being called *little*" (43; Dundes's emphasis).

The cultural historian Robert Darnton (1984) also prominently entered the debate about Red Riding Hood. Darnton criticized Erich Fromm for basing the symbolism he found in the story "on detail that did not exist in the versions known to peasants in the seventeenth and eighteenth centuries" (11). As Darnton noted, the Grimms' version that Fromm used was from a French Huguenot family, the Hassenpflugs, whose telling of the tale was based on Perrault's version, not on oral tradition. While Darnton was aware that we can have no direct knowledge of tales as told by peasants in the centuries to which he referred, still he argued that with the methods of folklorists and anthropologists some reconstruction of the way peasants told the tale in earlier times can be made. In his view, therefore, the versions collected from peasants beginning about the middle of the nineteenth century give a truer picture of how Red Riding Hood was told among peasants earlier.

My commentary, like Bettelheim's, emphasized instead the girl's relationship to her grandmother, especially as regards the gift of the red cap: "the grandmother's 'transformation' into the wolf, in the sense of his impersonation—and incorporation—of her, may hint at an equating of her sort of devotion [to the granddaughter] with that of a man. The girl's nickname, of course, derives from this very devotion on the grandmother's part, which in the Grimms' story is described in terms almost befitting a lover [...]" (McGlathery, 1991, 57).

Most recently, Jan Ziolkowski has argued (1992) that a brief medieval Latin story deserves serious consideration as an important ancestor of the Red Riding Hood tale. In the medieval story, after a five-year-old girl's godfather has given her a red wool tunic at her baptism, she is abducted by a wolf and taken to its lair to be eaten by its cubs. When the cubs are alone with the girl, they are prevented from harming her, by virtue of her baptism, and therefore instead try to caress her head, whereupon she admonishes them not to damage her red tunic, of which she is evidently quite proud.

Bluebeard

The story about the man who murdered a series of wives because they could not resist the temptation to open the door to a secret room is no longer so very well known, for one thing because it is deemed too gruesome these days for adaptation as children's literature. The Grimms, indeed, excluded it from their collection beginning with the second edition (1819) probably in part for that reason, though chiefly because they judged their version to be too much like Perrault's "La barbe bleue." Still less familiar in the United States is another story of the Bluebeard type, "Fitcher's Bird" (KHM 46), in which three sisters are abducted and successively put to the test of the forbidden door.

Regarding this latter story, Ernest Tonnelat noted that not until the Grimms' seventh edition (1857) was an explanation provided for why the third daughter, who tricks the murderer into believing that she has withstood the temptation, thereby gains complete power over him (1912, 138-39). In the earlier editions, she was simply the prospective bride who sets a condition on her acceptance of Fitcher's proposal of marriage. In the seventh edition, though, after he says, "You shall be my bride," it is related that "He now had no more power over her and had to do as she demanded." Although Tonnelat did not make the point, the Grimms' change was probably introduced to help readers understand that Fitcher, in becoming a bridegroom, became a prisoner of love and was therefore at his bride's mercy, as he then clearly proves to be.

Stories of the Bluebeard type were the subject of a dissertation by Emil Heckmann (1930). He argued that the type originated in mythological tales of death abducting young maidens and was then 'contaminated' by ballads about sexual murderers. In another study later in that decade, Josef Herzog (1938) compared the plot elements of various versions of the bluebeard tales, including those resembling the Grimms' "Fitcher's Bird." Then, in the post-World War II years, Paul Delarue published the first installment of a folkloristic study of the Bluebeard type (1952, 348-57).

Among the first interpretive commentary on the Grimms' "Fitcher's Bird" was Bruno Bettelheim's suggestion that the egg the girls must carry around with them at their abductor's house functions as "a symbol of female sexuality." Regarding the Bluebeard story, Bettelheim offered the more speculative view that "The key that opens the door to a secret room suggests associations to the male sexual organ, particularly in the first intercourse when the hymen is broken and blood gets on it [i.e., on the 'key']. If this is one of the hidden meanings, then it makes sense that the blood cannot be washed away: defloration is an irreversible event" (1976, 300-01). While Bettelheim's viewpoint was Freudian, H. H. Mowshowitz took an epistemological approach, arguing that the lesson the heroine in Perrault's version learns is the unreliability of sight (1979).

Unlike Mowshowitz, Maria Tatar did not quite see in the Bluebeard story a depiction of a philosophical issue; but she did argue that this type of tale was actually about "the heroine's quite legitimate *cognitive* curiosity (what does her husband have to hide?)" (Tatar's emphasis). In Tatar's view, "What Bettelheim and others do with few hesitations, reservations, and second thoughts is to turn a tale depicting the most brutal kind of sexual murders into a story about idle female curiosity and duplicity." Tatar observed that in the second of the two "morals" that Perrault appended to his version, it is implied that "Bluebeard [...] is the victim of sexual jealousy—hence his need to subject each successive wife to a test of absolute obedience," a test that "becomes as much [one] of fidelity as of obedience" (1988, 134-35).

In my commentary on Perrault's version, I agreed with Tatar that the bride wants to know what her husband has to hide: "What is clear, certainly, is the heroine's desire to know just what sort of man she has married, and specifically, what murderous crimes he has perhaps committed in view of the rumors she has heard about the disappearances of his former wives." My observation about the Grimms' version, "Blaubart," in which the bride has brothers and a widower father instead of a sister and a mother, was that the story became with the Grimms "as much a portrayal of devotion between a sister and her brothers as of a maiden's involvement with a beastly bridegroom" (McGlathery, 1991, 68). About the Grimms' "Fitcher's Bird," I agreed with Bettelheim that the eggs which the abducted girls are required to protect and carry around in their hand wherever they go symbolize female sexuality, but I found that "This otherwise nonsensical requirement is perhaps further evidence of the sorcerer's misogyny, in so far as eggs are associated with the female role in reproduction, and the dropping of this particular egg into the blood [on the floor] in the particular room serves as testimony to that sex's inability to withstand the urgings of curiosity" (71).

Sleeping Beauty
Second only to Little Red Riding Hood perhaps in the amount of critical commentary it has attracted, this story was the subject of an early essay by Friedrich Vogt (1896), who considered the versions

found in the collections of the Grimms, Perrault, and Basile to have originated in myths of the seasons, with the maiden's awakening from her long sleep betokening the arrival of springtime. Franz Kampers (1915), meanwhile, judged that the origin of the basic motifs in the story was to be found in the context of ancient ideas about the birth of the sun god from the womb of an earth goddess (187).

Concerning the idea, which Jacob Grimm had advanced in his notes to this tale, that it originated perhaps in connection with nordic tales about Sigurd's awakening of the slumbering valkyrie Brynhild, Robert Petsch (1917) agreed that there were "certain connections" between the two narratives but rejected any claim of direct descent. As Petsch observed, narratives of the Sleeping Beauty type were more common and more richly developed in countries outside the Germanic language area. In this connection, he noted that in these versions, "It is narrated [...] consistently, that the liberator makes love to her and that she bears him children, but that she is then horribly persecuted by his malevolent mother or by his first wife before she is [finally] saved" (81). Petsch argued, though, that the persecution of Sleeping Beauty in these versions derives from the Greek myth about "Thaleia, the daughter of Hephaistos, [...] who has to be hidden from the jealous eyes of Hera and who bore him twins"—a myth to which Basile's Sleeping Beauty story (*Pentamerone* V, 5) appears closely related, not least because of Basile's heroine being named Talia. Petsch contended, therefore, that another version lacking the persecution of the heroine explains the lack of that motif in both the story of Brynhild and in the Grimms' version of Sleeping Beauty. Petsch's intent was to counter the claim that the Grimms' version represents a shortening of Perrault's tale and other Romance versions through omission of the story's second half, which Petsch considered to be unmotivated by the events of the first half.

In a good study of the relationship between Perrault's version, "La belle au bois dormant," from which the type's English name is taken, and the Grimms' "Little Briar-Rose" ("Dornröschen," KHM 50), Alfred Romain (1933) showed how the Grimms, in the course of their editions of the collection, borrowed from Perrault's version where it suited them, while at the same time introducing changes of their own in accord with the German Biedermeier culture of their time. In particular, Romain found that they used Perrault's version where it was more concrete, dramatic, poetic, or the like, yet cast the family as that of a patriarchal German lord of the manor (*Gutsherr*) instead of a ruler of the Baroque period, and replaced erotic elements with an emphasis on the girl's spiritual virtue as the source of her appeal. Romain considered the Sleeping Beauty story to belong decidedly to literary as opposed to oral tradition, at least as far as its transmission in Germany was concerned.

In a psychoanalytic study that same year (1933), Steff Bornstein interpreted the Grimms' version as symbolizing a girl's psychic state in the transition to sexual womanhood, but also as reflecting a father's possessive love of his daughter. Bornstein judged that the girl experiences unconscious revulsion at the thought of marriage and the sexual act, while she at the same time harbors sexual curiosity. The role of the wise women in predicting the girl's fate at her birth, together with the role of the hag at the spinning wheel in the tower later, Bornstein saw as projecting the girl's feelings about her mother's feelings toward her. Bornstein based his interpretation largely on the assumption that the tale was invented by an adolescent girl. The spindle was associated symbolically with menstruation and defloration; the thorny hedge through which the young man must penetrate to reach her projects her enmity toward, and anxiety about, men; and the hundred-year-long sleep represents her progression from temporary rejection of sexuality and postponement of sexual involvement then to loss of virginity, marriage, and entry into womanhood. Bornstein supported his interpretation by referring to puberty rites among primitive peoples, especially as regards menstruation, defloration, removal of the clitoris, etc.

Bornstein's commentary was followed at the end of the 1930s by Bruno Jöckel's similarly Freudian interpretation. Jöckel, though, added a focus on the story's hints about the father's feelings toward the only daughter. Jöckel judged that the father harbors a romantic attachment to the daughter from the moment of her birth, with the result that "The girl is hindered by her own father in the development which would lead to another man [i.e., to a husband]" (1939, 44). Regarding the story's imagery, Jöckel argued that "The spindle is [...] a decidedly male symbol that refers directly to sexual intercourse" and that "climbing the staircase to the tower must render the girl giddy as with adolescents at the beginning of their sexual maturation" (46).

While Fritz Ernst's *Dornröschen in drei Sprachen* (1949) offered little more than texts of the Sleeping Beauty story from the collections of the Grimms, Basile, and Perrault in the respective languages, a subsequent essay by Jan de Vries (1958) compared the versions from those collections with the earliest recorded French example, *Perceforest,* from around 1340. De Vries approached the comparison in a folkloristic and philological manner, seeking to discern traces of the story's chief motifs in earlier literature, especially in medieval sources. His focus was on the question of the origins of the story, not interpretation.

De Vries's study was followed several years later by Max Lüthi's essay (1962b), which did address the question of the meaning of Sleeping Beauty. While granting that it was a love story focusing on the heroine's psychic development, Lüthi rejected the sexual terminology applied by psychoanalytic critics in favor of a vaguer formulation of the process as "the self-withdrawal of the young girl unto herself and the breaking of the spell through the youth's love." Lüthi found the story's ultimate object of depiction, indeed, to be "the endowment, menacing, paralyzation, and redemption not only of some girl or other but of mankind in general" (8).

Consideration of various possible interpretations of the story was offered by Barbara Bucknall in a 1975 essay on Perrault's version. She argued that many explanations—especially psychoanalytical ones—can be made, but since none will be exhaustive, no single interpretive view can be deemed correct. Bruno Bettelheim's Freudian interpretation then appeared the following year. In his view, "the central theme of all versions of 'The Sleeping Beauty' is that, despite all attempts on the part of parents to prevent their child's sexual awakening, it will take place nonetheless" (1976, 230-31). Like Jöckel earlier (1939), whom he did not cite, Bettelheim found "possible sexual connotations" in the role of the spindle in the Grimms' version (233). Also like Jöckel, Bettelheim saw hints of an erotic attraction between Sleeping Beauty and her father. Unlike Jöckel, though, Bettelheim judged these feelings to originate rather with the daughter: "We encounter here [...] the 'innocence' of the oedipal child, who feels no responsibility for what she arouses or wishes to arouse in the parent" (228). Bettelheim found this element to be suggested especially in Basile's version, "Sun, Moon, and Talia" (*Pentamerone* V, 5), where the father, thinking the daughter to be dead, departs, and she awakens only after she has been violated by a married man and has given birth to his twin children. As Bettelheim noted, "One king replaces another king in the same country; one king replaces another in Talia's life—the father king by the lover king. Might these two kings not be substitutes for each other at different periods in the girl's life, in different roles, in different disguises?" (228).

Instead of adopting Bettelheim's view, William Woods's interpretation was rather like an echo of Lüthi's more spiritual perspective, seeing Sleeping Beauty, and the Grimms' version in particular, as "a story of self-meeting, and its eternal promise is that of self-realization, the blossoming thorn, the curse turned to joy" (1978, 22). Ester Zago, though, commenting on Basile's version (*Pentamerone* V, 5), expressed the opinion that the Neapolitan author had deemphasized the theme of incest and illicit desire, compared with his possible sources, out of a personal reserve and discretion regarding sex that contrasted with his predilection for the scatological (Zago, 1981).

Jacques Barchilon, too (1990), pointed to the depiction of erotic desire in Basile's likely—direct or indirect—source, the prose novel *Perceforest* (1528), dating from the 14th century, which, Barchilon reported, was translated into Italian in 1558. In *Perceforest*, the Prince Charming figure, Troylus, violates the Sleeping Beauty Zellandine, who in this version is his fiancée. Troylus violates her, indeed, at the urging of Venus, who speaks with the voice of the lover's own erotic desire. As Barchilon observed, in *Perceforest* "It is, in sum, a matter of giving in to an erotic temptation" (22).

My commentary on the story focused on the father's devotion to the daughter: "depiction of the father as longing for a daughter becomes related to a crisis involving her eventual arrival at marriageable age" (McGlathery 1991, 98). I pointed to the doubling of this theme in Basile's version (*Pentamerone* V, 5), where we have "a similarly intense passion for the daughter on the part of another older man, a king who is unhappily married." Basile's version, moreover, "has the father and daughter [...] living together in a secluded sylvan palace, while Perrault and the Grimms have her living with both parents in the father's royal residence" (108). I commented, too, on the feelings of the fairies toward the baby daughter in the Grimm and Perrault versions, seeing them as identifying with the girl as an eventual object of erotic desire (117-19).

Snow White

While the Red Riding Hood and Sleeping Beauty stories have attracted the most critical commentary, Snow White is perhaps the most beloved tale in the United States, not least because Walt Disney chose it for his first feature-length animated film (1937). A geographical-historical study of some 70 variant versions, identifying constituent motifs and other elements, was done by Ernst Böklen (1910/15). Although Böklen, in his introduction to the second volume, expressed the conviction that "the explanation of the original sense of the transmitted stories is the main task of all study of fairy tale and myth" (1915, 1), he did not himself venture an interpretation. Among the earliest interpretive commentary was the heavily Freudian approach of Grant Duff (1934). Wilhelm Schoof, meanwhile, published an essay (1941) on the Grimms' "Sneewittchen" (*KHM* 53) to illustrate their development of a particular narrative style.

Bruno Bettelheim argued for a relationship between the stepmother's enticements and Snow White's becoming nubile. While she is with the dwarfs she "becomes an adolescent [...] [and] begins to experience the sexual desires which were repressed and dormant during latency. [...] The readiness with which Snow White repeatedly permits herself to be tempted by the stepmother, despite the warnings of the dwarfs, suggests how close the stepmother's temptations are to Snow White's inner desires" (1976, 211). The following year, N. J. Girardot, writing in the *Journal of American Folklore* (1977), interpreted the Snow White story as symbolically reflecting rites of initiation for females, in a social and religious context, as opposed to a strictly psychoanalytical or psychological sense. The tale was then chosen several years later by Hermann Bausinger (1980) to exemplify the problem of interpreting fairy tales generally, which he did by offering a critical discussion of interpretive positions on the tale to that time. A structural analysis of this tale type was attempted by Steven Swann Jones (1983).

For feminist critics, Snow White exemplifies how fairy tales assign to women subordinate roles in a male-dominated society. Sandra Gilbert and Susan Gubar traced the queen's envy of Snow White to her husband's valuing her for her beauty: "His, surely, is the voice of the looking glass, the patriarchal voice of judgment that rules the Queen's—and every woman's—self-evaluation. [...] the Queen has internalized the King's rules: his voice resides now in her own mirror, her own mind" (1979, 37-38). Regarding Snow White's role, Gilbert and Gubar argued that her life with the dwarfs "is an important part of her education in submissive femininity, for in serving them she learns essential lessons of service, of selflessness, of domesticity" (40). In seeming contradiction to this latter point by Gilbert and Gubar, Jennifer Waelti-Walters, a few years later, charged that the story is "an overt commercial for marriage, carrying with it the message that all that matters in a woman is her appearance. It is preferable that in all other aspects she be dead." Waelti-Walters's point is well taken that Snow White is after all considered to be dead when the prince falls in love with her: "The prince chooses the girl in the coffin—a picture in a frame—and it is only by accident that the apple is jolted out of her throat" (1982, 3).

In my commentary on the Grimms' "Little Snow White," I argued that the stepmother—in the Grimms' first edition of 1812 it is the girl's own mother—identifies vicariously with Snow White's blossoming maidenhood, as may be seen by the nature of her three temptations of the girl: a new bodice lace, a comb, and an apple (McGlathery, 1991, 121). I suggested, too, that the dwarfs' relationship to Snow White involves an avuncular sublimation of erotic desire: "They wish only to enjoy her charming presence as their maiden housekeeper and the cherished adornment of their bachelor household" (175).

Rumpelstiltskin

Of the best known Grimm tales, this one (KHM 55) is perhaps the most obscure and puzzling. The story attracted the early interest of an adherent of the British anthropological school, Edward Clodd, who followed his 1889 essay on "The Philosophy of Rumpelstiltskin" with a monograph on this story type entitled Tom Tit Tot: An Essay on Savage Philosophy in Folktale (1898). Clodd focused on the importance of names and the giving of names in connection with

Rumpelstiltskin, especially the primitive belief that to know someone's name is to have power over that person's body and soul. Names were used therefore in conjuring, casting evil spells, and the like. More recently, Josephine Bilz, writing from a pedagogical perspective, used this tale as her primary example for discussing folktale in relation to psychic processes associated with maturation (Bühler and Bilz, 1958).

Most of the critical attention devoted to Rumpelstiltskin, however, has remained concerned, as Clodd was, with survivals of primitive belief evident in the story. Gonthier-Louis Fink (1964) saw the tale as belonging originally to stories depicting the devil as stupid, especially in connection with the practice of exorcising him through addressing him by name. In stories about the devil as stupid, his aid is accepted, then he is cheated of his reward. Fink judged that Rumpelstiltskin's demand that the girl give him her firstborn child was a later development, belonging to the tale's evolution from one based on superstition to dramatic, realistic farce, with concurrent deepening of the psychological element. In his essay, Fink included consideration of a number of variants of the story, from both written and oral sources. Among other things, Fink suggested that the symbolism of the forfeits that the girl makes to Rumpelstiltskin in the Grimms' version indicates that the sprite is after her body. Fink attributed this symbolism to the Grimms, but he pointed also to the eroticism of some popular French versions in their scenes between the girl and the demon (62-63).

An intriguing, but extremely speculative proposition was put forth by Otto Kahn shortly after Fink's essay appeared. Kahn argued (1966/67) that in the Rumpelstiltskin story the little man was originally a member of an indigenous population in Europe that had been suppressed by the Indo-European invaders. The figure's strange name identified him as such, and thus had legal significance. Kahn maintained that originally Rumpelstiltskin's aim, as in some versions, was to marry the girl. The original goal was to improve his social and legal status. If the girl learned his name, she would recognize his inferior social station and not be bound by her promise. Kahn's view, moreover, was that the lore about dwarfs, wild men, etc., as exemplified in folktale, originated in the Indo-European experience of encountering the more primitive indigenous population.

While Max Lüthi, in an essay on Rumpelstiltskin (1971), offered an essentially structural analysis, Lutz Röhrich, like Fink before him, attempted to reveal the story's origins in earlier times through a philological approach. Röhrich (1972/73) focused on related narrative traditions in legends (*Sagen*) as well as *Märchen*. He concluded that Rumpelstiltskin's demand for a newborn baby paralleled that of the dwarfs in legends "who foist their own ugly children on people as changelings and steal human children for themselves." Moreover, Röhrich reported, in many versions the little man does not demand the baby but the girl herself, paralleling medieval legends in which "dwarfs steal human women in order to be joined with them." Indeed, according to Röhrich, Rumpelstiltskin's giving away his own secret is a motif "familiar from countless legends about changelings" (285). Noting that the allowance of a way out of an agreement was typical of stories about pacts with the devil, Röhrich, like Fink, saw Rumpelstiltskin as belonging to this type of story. But Röhrich (290-91) considered this aspect to be a later development in a tale that was originally about a dwarf instead of a devil, though that shift itself probably occurred quite early.

Like Röhrich, I addressed the question of why Rumpelstiltskin, in the Grimms' version, demands the newborn child of the miller's daughter. My answer was that he wants a child without having to engage in intercourse to obtain it. Like Fink, I viewed the game of forfeits that Rumpelstiltskin plays with the girl as suggesting that he is courting her; but my judgment was that, as a bachelor, he prefers flesh of her flesh to having her in the flesh herself (1991, 177-78).

C. Criticism on Other Stories

"The Holy Virgin's Child"
A story almost unknown in the United States, this tale has attracted scholarly interest especially for its different use of the motif of the forbidden room familiar from the Bluebeard story. A folkloristic study of the Grimms' version (*KHM* 3) and variations on it was done by Edeltraud Seifert-Korschinek (1952), who concluded that the original story was like the version the Grimms report about in their notes. In that variant, the forbidden room conceals four virgins dressed in black, not God, as in the Grimms' version; and the heroine's adoptive mother is not the Virgin Mary but simply a beautiful lady dressed in black. Seifert-Korschinek argued that the Grimms' version amounted to the making over of a secular story into a pious tale. Indeed, the secular version is the one the Grimms had in their manuscript of 1810. Several years after Seifert-Korschinek's monograph appeared, Marie-Louise von Franz (1955) published a Jungian interpretation of an Austrian version of the story, in which there is only one black virgin, not four. My interpretation of the girl's adventure with the forbidden door in the Grimms' version with the Holy Virgin—as well as in their variant with the four black virgins—was that it symbolically represents "the girl's arrival at nubility and the concomitant awakening desire and curiosity and beginning loss of sexual innocence" (McGlathery, 1991, 122-23; see also 133-34).

"Faithful John"
Like "The Holy Virgin's Child," this story (*KHM* 6) is not one familiar in the United States. Its importance in the history of European
folktale made it, however, the subject of a relatively early dissertation by Erich Rösch, published in the series Folklore Fellows Communications in 1928. Note of the story was taken, too, by Max Lüthi
in an essay (1975) investigating certain narrative possibilities ex-
ploited by several oral tellers of the story. Lüthi used these variants
to make the point that each version of a tale must be read closely
and critically as a work of literary art. My interpretation of both the
Grimms' version and the earlier one by Basile ("The Raven,"
Pentamerone IV, 9) was that we are dealing in each instance with
veiled, humorous depictions of bachelor resistance to thoughts of
marriage and, in particular, the wedding night. In Basile, the friend
who vicariously identifies with the bridegroom is the young man's
bachelor brother, while in the Grimms' story it is the bridegroom's
loyal servant, an old bachelor (McGlathery, 1991, 164-68).

"The Twelve Brothers"
  Also unfamiliar to Americans, this tale (*KHM* 9) revolves around
the enigmatic transformation of twelve brothers into ravens when
their sister picks twelve lilies. Pierre Bange (1979) offered a semiotic
analysis of the story, comparing the Grimms' manuscript version of
1810 with that in their second edition of 1819. While Bange only
touched upon the presence of a veiled theme of incest, I found the
devotion between the girl and her brothers to be the point of the
whole depiction. The brothers' transformation into ravens and their
resulting disappearance effectively remove them from the sister's
presence "as tangible objects of a forbidden love." This explains
"why the brothers are restored to human form only after the sister
is married, and why the happy ending consists in a resumption of
the siblings' blissful cohabitation, this time in circumstances ren-
dered more normal by the presence of the sister's spouse," whereas
before, the brothers and the sister had been living alone together in
a hut in the forest (McGlathery, 1991, 33-35). Ruth Bottigheimer
meanwhile asked, from a feminist viewpoint, why, since the
children's father was prepared to do away with the brothers when
the sister was born, in order to "allow for a greater accretion of
wealth and power to her," no further mention of this "female inheritance" is made in the story (1987, 38). My explanation was that "the
father's mad desire for a daughter introduces the underlying theme
of incestuous attachment," so that what follows is a case of 'like
father, like son' (McGlathery, 1991, 110).

"Little Brother and Little Sister"
Like "The Twelve Brothers," this tale (*KHM* 11) is a story of devotion between siblings of opposite sex. This sort of tale is especially

typical of the Grimms' collection, with Hansel and Gretel being the most famous example. From a psychoanalytic perspective, Bruno Jöckel cast doubt on the innocence of such attachment in "Little Brother and Little Sister." He found the focus of the story to be "the girl's fear of the brother's awakening sexuality," as projected in her visions of him being transformed into a wild animal that would tear her apart. The brother's transformation, then, into a tame fawn magically fulfills her wish to suppress "the little brother's male instincts" (1939, 117-18). My judgment was similar to Jöckel's. At the first two springs, "the brother manages to refrain from drinking, indicating perhaps that, for his part, he is able to resist any unconscious urge to ravish the sister—a potentiality that surely plays a role in the sister's unconscious erotic fantasies at least. When he does surrender to thirst at the third spring and is [...] transformed into a deer calf [...] his transformation has made it possible for the two of them to become [...] more intimate, because in his new magical form he is no longer so much a member of the opposite sex as a pet with whom the sister may exchange innocent affection [...]" (McGlathery, 1991, 39-40).

"The Fisherman and His Wife"
Concerning this well known story (*KHM* 19), about a woman's insatiable desire for wealth and status that does not stop short of wishing to be like God and about her husband's willing acquiescence, there has been little interpretive commentary. The literary reshaping of the tale was studied by Reinhold Steig (1903); and Heinz Rölleke (1973) reported the discovery of a letter from the author and scholar Friedrich von der Hagen to Achim von Arnim of May, 1808, which contains a version that came to him in a roundabout way. Motivated by Günter Grass's use of the story for the underlying motif of his novel *The Flounder* (*Der Butt*, 1977), Rölleke then published, under the title "The True Flounder" (*Der wahre Butt*, 1978a) a collection of versions of The Fisherman and His Wife from Germany and beyond.

"The Brave Little Tailor"
Like "The Fisherman and His Wife," this story (*KHM* 20) is one rather well known in the United States and yet one on which there has been a dearth of critical comment. Iring Fetscher, though, used it for exemplifying the Marxist approach to folktale (1980). The tailor, who slyly and shrewdly—and not without some self-deception—parlays his slaying of seven flies with a single swat ("seven with one blow") into marriage to a princess and inheritance of a kingdom was seen by Fetscher as representative of the bourgeoisie, with its upward mobility and growing power.

"Frau Holle"
While not very familiar to Americans, this tale (*KHM* 24) is among
the best known in Germany, not least because of its heavy moralism
and especially its teaching of household virtue. Like some other
quite popular tales, this story of a girl rewarded for her dutifulness
and industry poses few difficulties of interpretation. Gerhard Kahlo,
though, devoted a short essay to investigating the figure of Frau
Holle in relation to folklore (1957/58). At about the same time,
Warren Roberts focused on the type represented by this story in his
monograph *The Tale of the Kind and Unkind Girls* (1958).

"The Girl without Hands"
The long history of this tale (*KHM* 31), reaching back to the Middle
Ages, was traced in an early monograph by Heinrich Däumling
(1912). He concluded, from the literary versions he investigated,
that the medieval redactions were most often pious romances. The
incest theme he judged to be dominant, especially the father's lust
after his daughter, whereas in the Grimms' version it is instead the
father's demand that the girl have her hands cut off to prevent the
devil from taking him, because he had not made good on a promise.
Däumling found one strand of the tradition that avoided the theme
of incestuous desire by replacing it with an older woman's—usually
a mother's or stepmother's—envy of the girl's beauty, or of her
place in the father's affections. A feminist critic, Renate Meyer zur
Capellen (1980) used the tale as a point of reference for demonstrating how folktales can reflect men's feelings about women and
women's position in a male-dominated society. In comparing the
Grimms' pious version with Basile's "Penta the Handless"
(*Pentamerone* III, 2) about a brother's passionate attraction to his
sister, I observed that "In both tales the heroine lets her hands be
cut off in order to avoid evil, which is represented in Basile's tale by
the widower brother's demand that the sister marry him and in the
Grimms' version by the devil's claim on her father." I noted, too,
that the Grimms themselves, in their notes, refer to a version in
which the father wants to marry his daughter. When she refuses, he
cuts off not only her hands, but her breasts as well (McGlathery,
1991, 47, 111).

"The Table, the Ass, and the Stick"
A brief, heavily Freudian interpretation of this story (*KHM* 36) as
concerning the "phallic stage" was made by Roy Huss (1975). From
this perspective, the she-goat who figures at the beginning and end
of the story represents the otherwise absent mother of the three
boys; but the hidden reason the boys are driven from home by their
father is "for their autoeroticism rather than for their mother-lust,"
therefore "we may conclude that the tale dramatizes conflicts at the
phallic rather than at the Oedipal stage of development" (169).

"The Wedding of Mrs. Fox"
The reason that the widowed fox in this story (*KHM* 38) rejects all suitors until one arrives who has nine tails like her dead husband was judged by Ruth Bottigheimer to be that "Here we face the unambiguous double-entendre that Jacob Grimm denied, for in German tail (*Schwanz*) also means *cock* or *prick*" (1987, 160). Agreeing with this interpretation, I pointed to a likely instance of the same symbolism of an animal's tail in another Grimm story, "The Hare's Bride" (*KHM* 66; McGlathery, 1991, 64-65).

"The Juniper Tree"
Commenting on this tale (*KHM* 47), one of the best known in Germany, Bruno Jöckel focused on the devotion between the half-siblings and on the stepmother's resentment of her daughter's emotional ties to the stepbrother. Jöckel judged the shoes that the dead brother, resurrected as a bird, throws down to the sister to be "the symbol of love" (1939, 158). Subsequently, Wilhelm Schoof published a version of the story from the letters of the Grimms. There, whenever the girl goes to hear a beautiful bird's singing under the pear tree where she threw the stepbrother's bones, something beautiful always falls down for her (1953, 68-69). In making an interpretation very much like Jöckel's, I noted that in the version published by Schoof, the focus on the devotion between the brother and sister is especially strong (McGlathery, 1991, 29-30, 51 n. 2).

"King Thrushbeard"
Another of the stories that are well known in Germany, this tale (*KHM* 52) was the subject of a dissertation by Ernst Alfred Philippson (1923), in which he traced the type of the coy beauty to medieval sources. The first such version he discussed was a story "The Pear-Half," in which a girl's ridiculing of a man's table manners in halving a pear moves him to take revenge by seducing her. Commenting on the Grimms' version, Bruno Jöckel judged that the girl "feels herself still immature and seeks to compensate for this feeling of inferiority through a display of haughtiness" (1939, 59). My interpretation of the girl's rejection of all of her suitors was that it resulted, as in Basile's tales of this type (*Pentamerone* IV, 10 and V, 3), from resistance to the thought of marrying. As "the only daughter of an apparent widower" she "clings unconsciously to her proud position as maiden mistress of the castle" (McGlathery, 1991, 75).

"The Knapsack, the Little Hat, and the Little Horn"
A story about three brothers who set out to seek their fortunes, this tale (*KHM* 54) has attracted recent attention for its connection with social history. Michael Stolleis (1980) used it as an example of poor peoples' longing for salvation from material need. Similarly, Gonthier-Louis Fink (1988) discussed the Grimms' original version,

which they had from a retired soldier, as an example of how his way of telling stories reflected a particular social reality.

"Thousandfurs"
Virtually unknown in the United States and little known in Germany as well, this story (*KHM* 65) about a widower father's mad desire to wed his daughter was represented by similar ones in the earlier collections of Basile and Perrault. Commenting on the Grimms' version, Bruno Jöckel judged that the daughter's resistance to the proposal arises less from prohibitions against incest than her feeling that she cannot think about marriage until she possesses "the necessary maturity." Jöckel noted that the daughter does not reject her father's proposal of marriage outright, but instead asks him to provide her first with beautiful clothing. Her ultimate request is for a coat made of fur from all the animals in her father's kingdom, a request that in Jöckel's Freudian view "symbolizes the transformation into an animal which must necessarily precede arrival at maturity" (1939, 136). Heinz Rölleke showed (1972) that the Grimms' sketch of the plot in their manuscript of 1810—there it is a stepmother's jealousy, not a father's incestuous passion, that drives the girl from home—was based on a literary, not an oral source: the "Allerlei-Rauch" story told in the novel *Schilly* (1798) by Carl Nehrlich. René Demoris, meanwhile (1977), offered a sort of deconstructionist critique of Perrault's version (titled "Peau d'âne" or "Donkey Skin"), discussing matters of intertextuality and the range of associations of words and sounds.

Cay Dollerup and Ivan Reventlow argued (1986) that in the Grimms' 1812 version, the girl's father—a king—and the king whom the girl marries must be one and the same, since in that version, when the eventual husband is introduced as "the king, her fiancé," "the only fiancé we have heard about to that point is her father, whom she promised to marry" (21). In my commentary on the Grimms' version, I observed, like Jöckel, that instead of simply rejecting the father's marriage proposal immediately and completely, the daughter puts him off by asking for fine raiment. My judgment, though, was that the girl appears to test, unconsciously, the intensity of the father's passion for her, and thereby gains confidence in her ability to enchant men, as evidenced by her subsequent use of the beautiful dresses and the coat of many furs to win a husband (McGlathery, 1991, 101-02).

"Lucky Hans"
Hans Lüderssen used this tale (*KHM* 83) to discuss its relation to social history from a criminological viewpoint (1980).

"The Goose Girl"
Widely familiar to Americans as children's literature, this touching

tale (*KHM* 89) is about how the talking head of a princess's decapitated horse helps reveal the imposture of her chambermaid. Bruno Jöckel interpreted the story, in relation to psychoanalytical theory, as a depiction of the princess's transition from childhood to maturity. He noted the tender relationship between the old king, as prospective father-in-law, and the princess, which leads to the discovery of the chambermaid's posing as his son's intended. Jöckel found that relationship to show that "the child [in the princess] still predominates so much that she yearns for the paternal, but not the erotic, component in men." To further support this interpretation, Jöckel pointed to the princess's preventing the little boy with whom she tends geese from stealing a lock of her hair. The boy's desire is one that "belongs so properly to a small child, while in the transition period [to maturity that the girl is experiencing] hair is 'taboo.'" Moreover, Jöckel observed, after each of the boy's attempts on her tresses, the princess visits the head of the dead horse, showing in Jöckel's opinion the girl's retreat into childhood, into thoughts of her mother—who gave her the horse—and of home (1939, 150-51).

More recently, Ruth Bottigheimer, from a feminist viewpoint, suggested that the story contains survivals of belief in women's supernatural powers, since the chambermaid's imposture occurs after the princess has lost a handkerchief the mother had given her, and in view of the princess's ability to command the winds to protect her tresses from the boy: "it appears to me that the young girl's queenship is related both to her ability to conjure the elements and to the three drops of blood, which were to be of service to her on her journey. The supernatural power of the old queen's blood is demonstrated by the girl's loss of dominance directly following her loss of the handkerchief bearing the blood" (1980, 6-7). I found the story's point to be that in gaining a husband the princess "wins for herself a devoted father, to fill the lack she had suffered [—her mother was a widow—] and to compensate her for having had to leave her mother in order to go off to marry." Also, like Jöckel, I saw in the princess's prevention of the theft of her lock of hair evidence that she "is not unaware of her erotic appeal," and that there is a significant connection between the defense of her tresses and her visits to the talking head of the dead horse; for this practice results in the prospective father-in-law's discovery of the chambermaid's imposture (McGlathery, 1991, 148-49).

"The Poor Miller's Boy and the Cat"
An odd tale about a princess transformed as a cat who takes in a poor youth and marries him, this story (*KHM* 106) is essentially unknown to Americans. Ruth Bottigheimer called attention to the tale, commenting that "nearly every image and metaphor [in it] can be read erotically" and citing as examples the cat-princess's invitation to Hans to dance and, after he refuses, her order to "her feline

maids-in-waiting to take him to bed" (1987, 157-58). I read the story similarly, observing that "the princess is prepared from the outset to wait seven years before revealing her identity and making it to the altar" and that the reason may be that "the youth on whom she has set her cap is not yet fully grown, since at the end of the seven years the clothes he was wearing when he arrived at the castle no longer fit him" (McGlathery, 1991, 141).

"The Skilled Huntsman"
Another of the tales of love and marriage unfamiliar in the United States, this one (*KHM* 111) was among those chosen for comment by Bruno Jöckel as being of interest psychoanalytically. He noted the implication that the slumbering princess here has strong emotional ties to her father, as witnessed by the eventual suitor's finding her father's name on her right slipper and hers on the left, and the father's name on the right side of her neckerchief and hers on the left side. This discovery by the young man, Jöckel argued, helps explain why he then leaves instead of courting the princess. At the same time, as Jöckel observed, there are indications the father wants to marry off the daughter. Jöckel interpreted the father's having sewn up the slumbering daughter in her nightshirt as meaning that she should not "fall into a man's possession before her completed arrival at maturity" (Jöckel, 1939, 101-04).

As Maria Tatar recently pointed out, the Grimms relegated to their notes a version of this tale they had from Dorothea Viehmann, who was, as Tatar observed, their "favorite exhibit when it came to discoursing on the excellence of folk narrators." As Tatar reported, "Viehmann's version [...] relates that the story's hero enters a tower, discovers a naked princess asleep on her bed, and lies down next to her. After his departure the princess discovers to her deep distress and to her father's outrage that she is pregnant" (Tatar, 1987, 7). My conclusion about the veiled meaning of the Grimms' version was that the father may harbor an "anticipatory, vicarious identification with whoever is destined to become the lucky suitor." Moreover, the young man's failure to awaken and court the princess while yet taking with him "all three items with the father's name on them [...] indicates that [he] thinks of himself, if only unconsciously, as assuming the father's role as the maiden's fetishistic admirer, since slippers and neckerchiefs—not to forget nightshirts—belong to the more intimate sphere of a maiden's wardrobe" (McGlathery, 1991, 90-91).

"Ferdinand the Faithful and Ferdinand the Unfaithful"
Not familiar to Americans either, this intriguing tale (*KHM* 126) attracted deserved comment from Ruth Bottigheimer. Her interpretation of the queen's murder of her husband in order to marry

young Ferdinand is that, in view of the description of the king's lack of a nose, he "is missing something important, perhaps central [i.e., his male member], and the Queen can't say what it is" (1987, 160). My focus was instead on the youth's escape from the murderous queen into his devoted relationship with his talking horse, which in the end turns out to be a youth who had been under an evil spell. In my view, the magical queen's role is as "an object of bachelor anxiety about marrying" and that the horse "has represented Ferdinand's unreadiness for marriage all along." The horse was promised to him at his birth, as a magical gift from his godfather to be given to him when he reached fourteen, the age, as I remarked, "at which boys tend to form close relationships with members of their own gender in reaction to awakening desires that are urging them toward involvement with the opposite sex" (McGlathery, 1991, 170).

"Snow-White and Rose-Red"
The story is about the other Snow White—the one (*KHM* 161) who marries a prince who first appeared to her dressed as a bear, and whose sister marries the prince's brother—is not unknown in the United States. As Felix Karlinger showed (1963), this tale was taken over into oral tradition by storytellers in Sardinia. Karlinger's reference to this story as a "literary tale" (*Buchmärchen*) proved to be prophetic; for Heinz Rölleke subsequently pointed to a strong likelihood that the romantic part of the story was invented by Wilhelm Grimm, who thereby turned an account of the girls' involvement with a misogynous dwarf into a tale of love and marriage. In the notes, Grimm reported that while his source was Caroline Stahl's *Fabeln, Märchen und Erzählungen* (Nuremberg, 1818), he "told it, however, in my own way." In the revised and expanded version of the Grimms' notes, Johannes Bolte had suggested that the Grimms possibly took most of the rest of the story from some French tale of the eighteenth century or other (Bolte and Polívka, 1913-32, III, 259-60) ; but Heinz Rölleke's suggestion that Wilhelm invented this part seems more likely. As Rölleke demonstrated (1986b), Wilhelm Grimm's first version of the story, antedating that included in the third edition of 1837, was done as a contribution to Wilhelm Hauff's *Märchenalmanach* for the year 1827 (in Rölleke's essay, the texts of the two versions are printed side by side).

Regarding the interpretation of the story as told in the Grimms' collection, Karen Rowe referred to it as one of the tales that "mask latent incest as filial love and displace blatant sexual desires onto a substitute, such as a beast" (1979, 243-44). I, too, viewed the girls' relationship to the 'bear' as compensating them, at first, for the lack of a father and the absence of male companionship altogether. The avuncular friend becomes Snow-White's suitor. The dwarf's encounters with the girls, meanwhile, hint at the opposite pole in heterosexual relationships, that of older sisters with younger brothers, or the bachelor role of misogynist instead of avuncular friend. The relationship of the prince to the sisters, moreover, can be seen as showing how Wilhelm Grimm himself preferred to portray romantic love, since "except for his bear costume—which is so thin a disguise that it tears on a doorknob—the suitor behaves for all the world like an eligible bachelor of the Grimms' own Biedermeier time, class, and culture" (McGlathery, 1991, 60-61, 175-77, 190-91, 192-93).

"The Glass Coffin"

More even than "Snow-White and Rose-Red"—and much more clearly so— this story (*KHM* 163) is of decidedly literary origin. As the Grimms reported in their notes, their source was a novel of 1728. Hermann Hamann noted that the tone of the original was cruder, giving as an example the description of the unclad heroine in the glass coffin "'in which he saw an exceedingly beautiful and well-formed, entirely naked female person lying who was stretched out lengthwise'" (as quoted by Hamann, 1906, 83). Recently, Ruth Bottigheimer, from a feminist perspective, pointed to erotic elements that remained in the Grimms' version. Referring to the earlier episode of the stranger entering the heroine's bedroom, Bottigheimer found this depiction to be a "revelation of the young woman's vulnerability, that is, her powerlessness against an intrusion that can be read sexually as well as spatially [...]" (Bottigheimer, 1987, 77). My discussion of the story centered on the relationship between the brother and the sister, who have been living together alone for some time before the magical stranger enters their lives. I judged that "The magical stranger's role as presumptuous suitor, with the attendant transformation of the brother and the magical imprisonment of the sister [in the glass coffin of the title], is thus perhaps a projection of the siblings' guilt over an unconsciously incestuous attachment" (McGlathery, 1991, 42-45).

"The House in the Woods"

The handsome young prince in this story (*KHM* 169), who masquerades as an old hermit and has young girls sleep over at his house, attracted some recent critical attention. Ruth Bottigheimer noted that "this problematic action" of retiring together to the bedchamber "is cloaked with virtue." She found unconvincing the ostensible purpose of testing the girls' virtue by seeing which of them shows compassion for the man's animals: "the tale's sexuality shimmers palely and unmistakably through the veil behind which the unsatisfactory girls have been dumped" (Bottigheimer, 1987, 161-62). I saw the prince, instead, as plagued by misogynous fears, and viewed the curse placed on the prince by a witch as projecting his inward yearning "to be assured that the girl he married was thoroughly loving, not moved to kindness toward him out of a desire to marry a handsome prince." The prince, I concluded, was attracted to the girls because of the devotion they showed their father, by bringing his lunch out to the fields to him each day (McGlathery, 1991, 172).

"Spindle, Shuttle, and Needle"
Hermann Hamann showed that Wilhelm Grimm made significant changes in his source for this tale (*KHM* 188), which he took from Ludwig Aurbacher's collection of stories *Büchlein für die Jugend* (Stuttgart and Tübingen, 1834). The changes concerned the orphaned girl's desire to wed the prince. Wilhelm was responsible for the girl's blushing and for the commentary about, and portrayal of, her gazing after the prince, including her excuse to herself about why she went to the window (it was so hot in the room; whereas the heat she feels actually comes from her blushing). Also, in the Grimms' sources, the girl's incantation differs in that she does not so boldly express the wish to fetch the prince back once he has departed (Hamann, 1906, 97). In my commentary on the story, I saw the girl as the type of the "fetching maiden," who acts to win the man of her dreams, and viewed the magic of her spindle, shuttle, and needle as deriving their power from her deceased godmother and guardian's wishes for the girl, out of the godmother's unfulfilled desire as an old maid, and her consequent identification with the goddaughter's blossoming charms (she dies when the goddaughter is sixteen; McGlathery, 1991, 127, 142-43.)

"The Little Rabbit"
A folkloristic, geographical-historical study of this tale (*KHM* 191) was undertaken by Ingrid Hartmann-Ströhm. She judged that the story's original version must have been one in which the suitor is transformed into a flea, as opposed to the tiny rabbit in the Grimms' version (1953, 89). As the Grimms have it, the princess's bet with her suitors, ninety-nine of whom she has had put to death by decapitation and their heads mounted on stakes in front of her castle, is that they will not be able to hide themselves from her. The hundredth suitor, the youngest of three brothers who make the attempt, succeeds in hiding himself on her body, where she does not detect him. My interpretation of the princess's wagering of her maidenhood is that it depicts her crisis of having become nubile. She seems attracted to the youth, since he is the only suitor to whom she offers three chances to win. He gains entry into her castle because he manages to get transformed into a small pet, the little rabbit of the title. The girlish wish for a pet, instead of a lover, proves to be the princess's 'undoing': "The youngest brother has won because he

was able to hide himself on her body. It was this intimacy with a man the princess at once dreaded and desired" (McGlathery, 1991, 65-66).

"Dear Mili"
It is appropriate to conclude this survey of scholarly commentary on individual Grimm tales by noting the attention recently paid to a story that was not included in their collection, but is contained instead in a letter that Wilhelm wrote in 1816 to a certain "Mili," presumably a young admirer. Prominent attention was called to this tale by a front-page report in *The New York Times* by Edwin McDowell (1983), and subsequently by its publication as a children's book, translated by Ralph Manheim and illustrated by Maurice Sendak (Wilhelm Grimm, 1988). Between the appearance of the newspaper article and the publication of the book, John Ellis called into question the value and importance of this 'find.' Ellis argued that the story contained in the letter was not an authentic folktale, but was surely just concocted by Wilhelm Grimm: he "was writing a letter to a little girl, and to please her, on the spur of the moment made up a story in which she figured as the heroine. If he kept no other copy, he must have seen it as having no significance for the brothers' collection of fairy tales; and indeed, it has none" (1985, 89). While I wholeheartedly endorsed Ellis's opinion that the story was invented by Wilhelm Grimm, I differed with his verdict that the tale was unimportant with regard to *Grimms' Fairy Tales*. Precisely because the story appears to have been made up by Wilhelm, it gives us an example of his taste in storytelling. While, as I maintained, he "quite consciously modeled it on the type of pious tales, or 'Kinderlegenden,' as he called the section separately numbered at the end of the collection," in his mind he not only identified his correspondent with the story's heroine, but himself with St. Joseph, as the avuncular hermit with whom the girl resides alone in the forest for thirty years, during which she does not age and is protected from the ravages of war. Indeed, we may ask, I suggested, "Was Wilhelm secretly conveying [to the girl] [...] a sly confession of love and [...] a self-ironic image of himself?" (McGlathery, 1991, 191-93).

Epilogue

WHAT WILL THE FUTURE hold for study of folktale in general, and *Grimms' Fairy Tales* in particular? As with all predictions, any answer is more likely to be wrong than right. Who could have foretold, around 1960, that women's studies was about to arise, and with it feminist criticism of fairy tales? It is useful, nonetheless, to ask ourselves where criticism seems headed at this juncture, and which directions appear most viable and productive.

As we have seen, already at the start of their collecting of tales the Grimms were concerned that telling of traditional stories might be dying out. Now, almost two centuries later, there is still less reason to believe that so-called authentic folktales from oral tradition can be found, relatively untouched by influence from literary stories, or 'booktales,' as folklorists have come to call them. Even with regard to tales collected earlier, including the Grimms', there are few scholars who still believe that the stories can be traced to ancient origins, much less that reconstruction of an original or authentic form is possible. This resignation does not mean that individual motifs in the stories cannot be shown to have affinities with those found in ancient texts; on the contrary, there is every reason to believe that, not having been created out of thin air, folktales have taken their inspiration from a variety of available sources.

If the question is no longer where the story as a whole originated, and when, then what remains is—as Joseph Bédier insisted a century ago (1893)—to appreciate the texts for their poetic qualities and for what they tell us about the culture of the teller of the particular version. If such be the aim and motivation of the folklorist, then tales recorded and collected even today are important in their own right, regardless of whether they are clearly derived from 'booktales.' From this viewpoint, indeed, how the story is told is as important as what the story is, hence an increased interest among folklorists in studying storytelling as a performing art.

Just as the Grimms prominently raised the question of authenticity in oral tradition, they also perceived, as we have seen, a need to define fairy tale as a genre within folk narrative, especially vis-à-vis legend. At the same time, the Grimms broadened the compass of the genre by including in their collection fables, pious stories, merry tales, and other types of narrative not compatible with 'fairy tale' as it had been defined by the stories published by Perrault and his contemporaries a century before. As we have seen, attempts at determining what is or is not a *Märchen* have been common in this century, particularly among German scholars. Despite their best efforts, these critics cannot be said to have answered the question of genre satisfactorily. The matter remains open for debate.

The question of genre interested literary scholars more than it did folklorists; and literary scholars, starting around the beginning of this century, were the ones who came to write about a specifically Grimmian genre. In this form, the question posed was indeed the decidedly literary one of how the Grimms shaped their tales, and why. Although a good deal of widely accepted commentary on this score has been produced over the course of this century, many questions remain. Above all, as Heinz Rölleke has urged (1986a), each of the Grimms' tales deserves close study regarding its relation to its sources, wherever they can be determined, and to the changes the Grimms made in the course of the editions of their *Children's and Household Tales* during their lifetimes.

Whether or not the Grimms' tales—and indeed those of Perrault and Basile before them—demonstrate the existence of a broad oral narrative tradition among the 'folk' is a question not likely to be decided beyond reasonable doubt. While there is good evidence that various types of storytelling were practiced, it is less than certain that the type of narrative we have come to call fairy tale was widely told. As we have seen, Manfred Grätz argued (1988) that, in the case of Germany, the opposite appears to have been true, at least up until shortly before the time of the Grimms' collection. There is opportunity, though, for much further investigation of published and unpublished sources with regard to this question, including examination of correspondence between individuals in earlier centuries, as well as of literary works, broadly defined. Meanwhile, scholars and other critics should refrain from claiming—explicitly or implicitly—to know the answer.

As we have seen, the open question whether fairy tales derive from oral tradition has implications for psychoanalytical and other ideological critics. If the tales are possibly literary inventions, then they may need to be seen as products of individual minds, not of a collective unconscious or subconscious. If the tales are products of an unconscious, then a collective one only in the sense that the individual unconscious in understood to participate in that whole. In any case, if psychoanalytical critics are to be taken seriously by those who put little or no stock in the theories underlying that approach, they will need to be less inclined to make the circular argument that because of the truth of those theories the tales must somehow accord with them. This is not to deny the legitimacy of studies that limit themselves to showing what the meaning of a story is when one theoretical viewpoint or another is employed. All ideological critics—nationalists, anthroposophists, existentialist, Marxists, platonic idealists, and others—need to be held to these same standards if they wish to be taken seriously by non-believers.

Ideological critics—and the 'meteorological' school of fairy-tale interpretation before them—can be credited with posing the question of the stories' meaning, which folklorists and philologists have tended to avoid. As Lutz Röhrich argued (1984), echoing the point made by some other scholars before him, the question of meaning has to be raised, because it is the ultimate issue. Why study the stories if we are not going to try to understand them? The meteorological critics, in trying to identify the characters in the stories with heavenly bodies or the seasons, assumed that the tales as we have them derive from prehistoric sources; and the ideological critics after them have tended to make the same romantic assumption that the tales are products of a collective mind or metaphysical consciousness. What is needed now, in seeking to understand the tales, is to start with the individual text and to discuss first its meaning as a narrative whole. The same should be done then for each and every version of the same story, respecting the fact that even small differences between one text and another—or even between two oral performances of the same text—can result in significant, or even complete, changes in meaning.

Studying the meaning of a text in isolation from other texts, as a self-contained poetic product, is only a beginning, of course. The meaning found in a particular text needs to be compared with that found in other texts that represent versions of the same story. Alan Dundes is right to insist (1988) that versions recorded from oral tradition need to be studied, not just those found in 'booktales.' Dundes's search for an authentic, or composite, version to interpret, however, marks a return to, or continuation of, earlier belief that such determinations are possible. What needs to be done instead is to compare shifts in meaning between different versions, leaving aside the question of authenticity. Moreover, versions of a particular tale need to be compared, in their depictions and meanings, with versions of other tales to find whether such depictions and meanings prove to be characteristic of fairy tale as a genre or tradition— an attempt I undertook with regard to stories of love and marriage when I wrote about *Fairy Tale Romance* (1991).

At present, study of meaning in fairy tales is dominated by feminist criticism. Here the question is legitimately asked, how fairy tales as we have them bear the stamp of a society and culture that can be described as patriarchal. As we have seen, the most speculative feminist approach is that which, contending as the Grimms had done that the stories are of ancient origin, claims them to date from prehistoric matriarchal societies. More widely accepted is the view that there was indeed a tradition of women storytellers, as suggested by the proverbial reference to 'old wives tales.' At the same time, feminist critics are wont not to claim the classic 'booktales' as women's literature, seeing them—whether invented or told by women or not—as being too heavily influenced by the male-dominated culture in which they arose—and influenced, moreover, also by male editors and adapters like Basile, Perrault, and the Grimms. In the—legitimate—feminist view, women are depicted in the tales as men want them to be, or as women have thought of themselves considering their traditional position in a patriarchal culture and society.

Female characters, of course, do play a major, and often leading, role in fairy tales. Feminist criticism, understandably, focuses on types of control and victimization of women as reflected in depictions of these female figures. For women's studies, however, as distinguished from feminism in a narrower sense, and for historians and literary critics and scholars generally, it should be important to understand the role of the female figures also in the context of the individual stories as a whole, in order to form a more complete picture of women as objects of poetic fantasy in given literary traditions in various cultures at different times. What are the motivations of the women in fairy tales? To what extent are they the same or different from the men? Are these motivations or urges such that any of us, regardless of gender, can identify with them? Can one speak here of shared passions not specific to gender, but common to human beings the world over and for all times?

Feminist criticism has participated in, and contributed to, the decidedly historical approach that has partially characterized literary studies of the past several decades, a trend especially pronounced in the study of German literature. To a considerable extent, this shift toward 'historicity' represented a turning away from psychoanalytical, existential, and aesthetic or platonic approaches, which had in common lesser regard for historical contexts. These latter approaches sought to find values or meanings in literature for all times. What is now called the 'New Historicism' has its roots in the liberation movements and student revolts of the 1960s and 1970s, with their more or less Marxist theoretical underpinnings. The aim in this method is to fit the literary work into the historical context in which it arose. One of the difficulties with this approach is that the view of history taken, explicitly or implicitly, may have a narrow ideological base that militates against acceptance of such studies' findings by any but the believers. Another problem is that, even in studies without strong ideological commitment, the critics may be so concerned to match historical facts and perceptions with elements in the literary text that they lose sight of the poetic work as a whole. Moreover, poetic literature as an art has something of a history of its own, in addition to its topical and other contemporary references. Poetic works cannot be properly understood without regard to such artistic traditions, which have a degree of timelessness, if not immortality.

The 'new historical' approach to literature has often been related to liberationists' efforts to broaden the so-called 'canon' of literary classics. Most everyone agrees, of course, that works considered to have little poetic merit or aesthetic interest may yet represent important historical documents. It is reasonable to argue, though, that works which have only historical interest and no artistic merit should not be held up as literary classics. Without a spark of literary genius, poetic masterpieces cannot be produced. Literary classics stand above their times, however much they may reflect them. The stories in the Grimms' collection which have become especially beloved have that spark of genius, which is to say perhaps no more than that they depict for us, in interesting and intriguing ways, timeless things about ourselves as human beings. Study of the Grimms' *Children's and Household Tales* as a mirror of their times needs to continue; but we must not forget to ask, too, what the stories tell us about our common humanity and how such depiction is achieved artistically.

Works Cited

EDITIONS OF GRIMMS' FAIRY TALES

During the Grimms' Lifetime:

The Full Collection (Große Ausgabe)

1812. *Kinder- und Haus-Märchen. Gesammelt durch die Brüder Grimm.* Berlin: Realschulbuchhandlung.

1815. *Kinder- und Haus-Märchen. Gesammelt durch die Brüder Grimm.* 2. Band. Berlin: Realschulbuchhandlung.

1819. *Kinder- und Haus-Märchen. Gesammelt durch die Brüder Grimm.* 2nd rev. and exp. ed. 2 vols. Berlin: Reimer.

1822. *Kinder- und Haus-Märchen. Gesammelt durch die Brüder Grimm.* 3. Band. Berlin: Reimer.

1837 *Kinder- und Haus-Märchen. Gesammelt durch die Brüder Grimm.* 3rd rev. and exp. ed. 2 vols. Göttingen: Dieterich.

1840. *Kinder- und Haus-Märchen. Gesammelt durch die Brüder Grimm.* 4th rev. and exp. ed. 2 vols. Göttingen: Dieterich.

1843. *Kinder- und Haus-Märchen. Gesammelt durch die Brüder Grimm.* 5th rev. and exp. ed. 2 vols. Göttingen: Dieterich.

1850. *Kinder- und Haus-Märchen. Gesammelt durch die Brüder Grimm.* 6th rev. and exp. ed. 2 vols. Göttingen: Dieterich.

1856. *Kinder- und Haus-Märchen. Gesammelt durch die Brüder Grimm.* 3. Band. 3rd ed. Göttingen: Dieterich.

1857. *Kinder- und Haus-Märchen. Gesammelt durch die Brüder Grimm.* 7th rev. and exp. ed. 2 vols. Göttingen: Dieterich.

The Shorter Collection (Kleine Ausgabe)

1825. *Kinder- und Haus-Märchen. Gesammelt durch die Brüder Grimm.* Kleine Ausgabe. Berlin: Reimer. New printings: 1833, 1836, 1839, 1841, 1843, 1844, 1846.

1850. *Kinder- und Haus-Märchen. Gesammelt durch die Brüder Grimm.* Kleine Ausgabe. 8th ed. Berlin: Duncker. New printings: 1853, 1858.

Selected Subsequent Editions:

1897. *Kinder- und Haus-Märchen. Gesammelt durch die Brüder Grimm.* Große Ausgabe. 29th ed. Ed. Herman Grimm. Berlin: Hertz.

1912. *Kinder- und Haus-Märchen. Gesammelt durch die Brüder Grimm.* Kleine Ausgabe. 50th ed. Ed. Reinhold Steig. Gütersloh: Bertelsmann.

1913. *Die Kinder- und Hausmärchen der Brüder Grimm in ihrer Urgestalt.* Ed. Friedrich Panzer. 2 vols. Munich: Beck.

1924. *Die Märchen der Brüder Grimm in der Urform nach der Handschrift.* Ed. Franz Schultz. Offenbach am Main: Klingspor.

1927. *Märchen der Brüder Grimm: Urfassung nach der Originalhandschrift der Abtei Ölenberg im Elsaß.* Ed. Joseph Lefftz. Schriften der Elsaß-Lothringischen Wissenschaftlichen Gesellschaft zu Straßburg: Reihe C, 1. Heidelberg: Winter.

1957. *Westfälische Märchen aus dem Nachlaß der Brüder Grimm.* Ed. Karl Schulte-Kemminghausen. 2nd ed. Münster: Aschendorff, 1963. Title of 1st ed.: *Von Königen, Hexen und Allerlei Spuk: Beiträge des Droste-Kreises zu den Märchen und Sagen der Brüder Grimm.*

1975. *Die älteste Märchensammlung der Brüder Grimm: Synopse der handschriftlichen Urfassung von 1810 und der Erstdrucke von 1812.* Ed. Heinz Rölleke. Biblioteca Bodmeriana: Texte, 1. Cologny-Genève: Fondation Martin Bodmer.

1977. *Märchen aus dem Nachlaß der Brüder Grimm.* Ed. Heinz Rölleke. Wuppertaler Schriftenreihe Literatur, 6. 3rd rev. ed. Bonn: Bouvier, 1983. 2nd ed. 1979.

1980. *Kinder- und Hausmärchen. Ausgabe letzter Hand mit den Originalanmerkungen der Brüder Grimm [und] mit einem Anhang sämtlicher, nicht in allen Auflagen veröffentlichter Märchen und Herkunftsnachweisen.* Ed. Heinz Rölleke. 3 vols. Reclams Universal-Bibliothek, 3191-93. Stuttgart: Reclam.

1982. *Kinder- und Hausmärchen.* 2nd exp. and rev. ed. of 1819. Ed. Heinz Rölleke. 2 vols. in 1. Cologne: Diederichs.

1986. *Kinder- und Hausmärchen. Gesammelt durch die Brüder Grimm. Vergrößerter Nachdruck der zweibändigen Erstausgabe von 1812 und 1815 nach dem Handexemplar des Brüder Grimm-Museums Kassel mit sämtlichen handschriftlichen Korrekturen und Nachträgen der Brüder Grimm sowie einem Ergänzungsheft: Transkriptionen und Kommentare.* Ed. Heinz Rölleke with Ulrike Marquardt. 2 vols. + supp. Göttingen: Vandenhoeck & Ruprecht.

1988. Grimm, Wilhelm. *Dear Mili.* Illustrated by Maurice Sendak and translated by Ralph Manheim. New York: Farrar, Straus, Giroux.

SELECTED EDITIONS OF GIAMBATTISTA BASILE'S TALES

1634/1636. *Lo cunto de li cunti: Trattenemiento de li peccerille.* 2 vols. Naples.

1846. *Der Pentamerone oder das Märchen aller Märchen.* Trans. Felix Liebrecht. Preface by Jacob Grimm. Breslau: Max. Reprint. 2 vols. in 1. Hildesheim and New York: Georg Olms, 1973.

1925. *Il Pentamerone ossia la fiabe delle fiabe: Tradotta dall'antico dialetto napoletano e corredata di note storiche.* Ed. and trans. Benedetto Croce. Bari: Laterza. Reprint 1957.

1927. *Il Pentamerone: or The Tale of Tales.* Trans. Richard Burton. New York: Boni & Liveright.

1932. *The Pentamerone of Giambattista Basile: Translated from the Italian of Benedetto Croce.* Ed. N. M. Penzer. 2 vols. London: Bodley Head; New York: Dutton.

1976. *Lo cunto de li cunti: overo, Lo trattenemiento de peccerille; Le Muse napolitane e le Lettere.* Ed. Mario Petrini. Scrittori d'Italia, 260. Rome: Laterza.

1986. *Lo cunto de li cunti. / Il Racconto dei racconti ovvero Il Passatempo per i più piccoli.* Ed. and trans. Michele Rak. Milan: Garzanti.

SELECTED EDITIONS OF CHARLES PERRAULT'S TALES

1695. *Contes de ma mère l'oye.* Paris: Coignard.

1697. *Histoires ou contes du temps passé, avec des moralitez.* Paris: Barbin. Reprint. Introd. Jacques Barchilon. Geneva: Slatkine, 1980.

1956. *Tales of Mother Goose: The Dedication Manuscript of 1695, Reproduced in Collotype Facsimile with Introduction and Critical Text.* Vol. 1: *Text;* Vol. 2: *Facsimile.* Ed. Jacques Barchilon. New York: Pierpont Morgan Library.

1957. *The Fairy Tales of Charles Perrault.* Introd. and trans. Geoffrey Brereton. Edinburgh: Penguin Books.

1960. *The Authentic Mother Goose.* Introd. Jacques Barchilon and Henry Pettit. Denver: Allen Swallow. Facsimile reprint of Charles Perrault, *Histories or Tales of Past Times.* Trans. Robert Samber. London: Pote, 1729.

1967. *Contes: Textes établis, avec introduction, sommaire biographique, bibliographie, notices, relevé de variantes, notes et glossaire.* Paris: Garnier.

1977. *The Fairy Tales of Charles Perrault.* Ed. and trans. Angela Carter. London: Victor Gollancz.

WORKS CITED, IN CHRONOLOGICAL ORDER

The following abbreviations are used throughout:
FFC = Folklore Fellows' Communications
Fabula = Fabula: Zeitschrift für Erzählforschung
Imago = Imago: Zeitschrift für Anwendung der Psychoanalyse auf die Natur- und Geisteswissenschaften

1845/1856. Bechstein, Ludwig. *Deutsches Märchenbuch | Neues Märchenbuch.* In *Sämtliche Märchen.* Ed. Walter Scherf. Munich: Winkler, 1965.

1851. Wolf, J. W. *Deutsche Hausmärchen.* Göttingen and Leipzig: Dieterich. Reprint Hildesheim and New York: Olms, 1972.

1852. Meier, Ernst Heinrich. *Deutsche Volksmärchen aus Schwaben.* Stuttgart: Scheitlin. Reprint Hildesheim and New York: Olms, 1971.

1855-63. Afanasyev, A. N. *Narodnye russkie skazki.* Ed. V. J. Propp. 3 vols. Moscow: Gosudarstvjennoje Izdatjeljstvo Chudojestvjennoj Literatury, 1957.

1859. Benfey, Theodor, ed. and trans. *Panchatantra: Fünf Bücher indischer Fabeln, Märchen und Erzählungen.* Leipzig: Brockhaus.

1865. Tylor, Edward Burnett. *Researches into the Early History of Mankind and the Development of Civilization.* London: Murray. 3rd rev. ed. 1878. (See esp. ch. 9: "Geographical Distribution of Myths.")

1871. Tylor, Edward Burnett. *Primitive Culture: Researches into the Development of Mythology, Philosophy, Religion, Language, Art and Custom.* 2 vols. London: Murray. 5th ed. 1913.

1879. Deulin, Charles. *Les Contes de ma mère l'Oye avant Perrault.* Paris: E. Dentu. Reprint Geneva: Slatkine, 1969.

1881. Tylor, Edward Burnett. *Anthropology.* London: Macmillan.

1883. Linnig, Franz. *Deutsche Mythen-Märchen: Beitrag zur Erklärung der Grimmschen Kinder- und Hausmärchen.* Paderborn: Schöningh.

1887. Lang, Andrew. *Myth, Ritual and Religion.* 2 vols. London: Longmans, Green and Co. Reprint of 1906 edition. New York: AMS Press, 1968.

1889. Clodd, Edward. "The Philosophy of Rumpelstiltskin." *Folk-Lore Journal* 7: 135-63.

1890/1894. Jacobs, Joseph. *English Fairy Tales.* London: Nutt; *More English Fairy Tales.* London: Nutt. Reprint (of 3rd ed. London: Putnam, 1898) New York: Dover, 1967.

1890. Frazer, James George. *The Golden Bough.* 3rd ed. 13 vols. London and New York: Macmillan, 1911-36.

1891. Cox, Marian Roalfe. *Cinderella: Three Hundred and Forty-Five Variants of Cinderella, Catskin, and Cap o' Rushes, Abstracted and Tabulated, with a Discussion of Mediaeval Analogues, and Notes.* Introd. Andrew Lang. Publications of the Folk-Lore Society, 31. London: The Folk-Lore Society. Reprint Nendeln/Liechtenstein: Kraus, 1967.

1891. Delaporte, P. Victor. *Du merveilleux dans la littérature française sous le règne de Louis XIV.* Paris: Retaux-Bray. Photo-reprint. Geneva: Slatkine, 1968.

1893. Bédier, Joseph. *Les Fabliaux: Études de littérature populaire et d'histoire littéraire du moyen âge.* Bibliothèque de l'École des Hautes Études: Sciences Philologiques et Historiques, 98. Paris: Bouillon.

1894. Benfey, Theodor. *Kleinere Schriften zur Märchenforschung.* Ed. Adalbert Bezzenberger. 2 vols. Berlin: Reuther. Reprint 2 vols. in 1. Hildesheim: Olms, 1975.

1894. Köhler, Reinhold. *Aufsätze über Märchen und Volkslieder.* Eds. Johannes Bolte and Erich Schmidt. Berlin: Weidmann.

1896. Vogt, Friedrich. "Dornröschen - Thalia." In *Beiträge zur Volkskunde: Festschrift für Karl Weinhold.* Germanistische Abhandlungen, 12. Breslau: Koebner, 195-237. Reprint Hildesheim: Olms, 1977.

1897. Arfet, P. *Das Motiv von der untergeschobenen Braut in der internationalen Erzählungsliteratur.* Diss. Rostock 1897. Schwerin: Bärensprung.

1897. Grimm, Herman. "Die Brüder Grimm und die Kinder- und Hausmärchen." In Herman Grimm, *Beiträge zur Deutschen Culturgeschichte.* Berlin: Hertz. 214-47.

1898. Clodd, Edward. *Tom Tit Tot: An Essay on Savage Philosophy in Folktale.* London: Duckworth. Reprint Detroit: Singing Tree, 1968.

1898. Köhler, Reinhold. *Kleinere Schriften zur Märchenforschung.* Ed. Johannes Bolte. Weimar: Felber. (Vol. 1 of his *Kleinere Schriften.* Ed. Johannes Bolte. 3 vols. Berlin: Felber, 1898-1900.)

1898. Lang, Andrew. *The Making of Religion.* London: Longmans, Green and Co.

1900. Petsch, Robert. *Formelhafte Schlüsse im Volksmärchen.* Berlin: Weidmann.

1901. Becker, Marie Luise. *Die Liebe im deutschen Märchen.* Leipzig: Seemann.

1901. Steig, Reinhold. "Zur Entstehungsgeschichte der Märchen und Sagen der Brüder Grimm." *Archiv für das Studium der neueren Sprachen und Literaturen* 107: 277-310.

1903/1906. Singer, Samuel. *Schweizer Märchen: Anfang eines Kommentars zu der veröffentlichten Schweizer Märchenliteratur.* 2 vols. Untersuchungen zur neueren Sprach- und Literaturgeschichte, 3, 10. Berne: Francke. Reprint Munich-Pullach: Verlag Dokumentation, 1971.

1903. Steig, Reinhold. "Literarische Umbildung des Märchens vom Fischer und siner Fru." *Archiv für das Studium der neueren Sprachen und Literaturen* 110 [= n.s. 10]: 8-19.

1904. Weber, Ludwig Felix. *Märchen und Schwank: Eine stilkritische Studie zur Volksdichtung.* Diss. University of Kiel 1904. Kiel: Fiencke.

1905. Panzer, Friedrich. *Märchen, Sage und Dichtung.* Munich: Beck.

1906. Hamann, Hermann. *Die literarischen Vorlagen der Kinder- und Hausmärchen und ihre Bearbeitung durch die Brüder Grimm.* Palaestra, 47. Berlin: Mayer & Müller.

1907. Aarne, Antti. *Vergleichende Märchenforschungen.* Helsingfors: Finnische Literaturgesellschaft.

1907. Benz, Richard. *Märchen und Aufklärung im 18. Jahrhundert: Eine Vorgeschichte zur Märchendichtung der Romantiker.* Diss. University of Heidelberg n.d. Gotha: Perthes.

1907. Krohn, Kaarle. *Vergleichende Märchenforschung.* Helsingfors: Finnische Literaturgesellschaft.

1908. Riklin, Franz. *Wunscherfüllung und Symbolik im Märchen.* Vienna and Leipzig: Hugo Heller. Partial reprint in Laiblin, ed. 1969, 13-55. Translated by William A. White as *Wish-Fulfillment and Symbolism in Fairy Tales.* Nervous and Mental Disease Monograph Series, 21. New York: The Nervous and Mental Disease Publishing Company, 1915.

1908/1913. Steiner, Rudolf. *Märchendichtungen im Lichte der Geistesforschung: Öffentlicher Vortrag, Berlin, 6. Februar 1913; Märchendeutungen, Vortrag vor Mitgliedern der Anthroposophischen Gesellschaft Berlin, 26. Dezember 1908.* Basel: Zbinden & Hügin, 1942. 3rd ed. Ernst Weidmann, ed. Dornach (Switzerland): Rudolf Steiner Nachlaßverwaltung, 1960. Translation of the 1908 lecture into English as *The Interpretation of Fairy Tales.* New York: Anthroposophic Press, 1929. Also London: Steiner, 1943.

1909. Olrik, Axel. "Epische Gesetze der Volksdichtung." *Zeitschrift für Deutsches Altertum und Deutsche Literatur* 51: 1-12.

1909. Thimme, Adolf. *Das Märchen.* Handbücher zur Volkskunde, 2. Leipzig: Heims.

1910. Aarne, Antti. *Verzeichnis der Märchentypen.* FFC, 3. Helsinki: Suomalaisen Tiedeakatemian Toimituksia.

1910/1915. Böklen, Ernst. *Sneewittchenstudien.* 2 vols. Leipzig: Hinrichs.

1911. Forke, Alfred. *Die indischen Märchen und ihre Bedeutung für die vergleichende Märchenforschung.* Berlin: Curtius.

1911. von der Leyen, Friedrich. *Das Märchen: Ein Versuch.* Leipzig: Quelle & Meyer. 4th rev. ed., with Kurt Schier. Heidelberg: Quelle & Meyer, 1958.

1912. Däumling, Heinrich. *Studie über den Typus des Mädchens ohne Hände innerhalb des Konstanze-Zyklus.* Diss. University of Munich 1912. Munich: Gerber.

1912. Löwis of Menar, August von. *Der Held im deutschen und russischen Märchen.* Diss. University of Berlin 1912. Jena: Diederichs.

1912. Tonnelat, Ernest. *Les contes des frères Grimm: Études sur la composition et le style du recueil des* Kinder- und Hausmärchen. Paris: Colin.

1913. Aarne, Antti. *Leitfaden der vergleichenden Märchenforschung.* FFC, 13. Helsinki: Suomalainen Tiedeakatemia / Academia scientificarum fennica.

1913-32. Bolte, Johannes, and Georg Polívka. *Anmerkungen zu den Kinder- und Hausmärchen der Brüder Grimm.* 5 vols. Leipzig: Dieterich. Reprint Hildesheim: Olms, 1963.

1915. Bolte, Johannes. "Deutsche Märchen aus dem Nachlaß der Brüder Grimm." *Zeitschrift des Vereins für Volkskunde* 25: 31-51; 372-80.

1915. Kampers, Franz. "Das Märchen vom Dornröschen." *Mitteilungen der Gesellschaft für schlesische Volkskunde* 17: 181-87.

1917. Petsch, Robert. "Dornröschen und Brynhild." *Beiträge zur Geschichte der deutschen Sprache und Literatur* 42: 80-97.

1917. Spieß, Karl. *Das deutsche Volksmärchen*. 2nd ed. Aus Natur und Geisteswelt: Sammlung wissenschaftlich-gemeinverständlicher Darstellungen, 587. Leipzig and Berlin: Teubner, 1924.

1918. Bühler, Charlotte. *Das Märchen und die Phantasie des Kindes*. Zeitschrift für angewandte Psychologie, supps. 17. Leipzig: Barth.

1919. Rank, Otto. *Psychoanalytische Beiträge zur Mythenforschung: Gesammelte Studien aus den Jahren 1912 bis 1914*. Internationale Psychoanalytische Bibliothek, 4. Leipzig and Vienna: Internationaler Psychoanalytischer Verlag.

1921. Berendsohn, Walter A. *Grundformen volkstümlicher Erzählerkunst in den Kinder- und Hausmärchen der Brüder Grimm: Ein stilkritischer Versuch*. Habilitationsschrift University of Hamburg 1920. Rev. reprint Wiesbaden: Sändig, 1968.

1922. Cosquin, Emmanuel. *Études folkloriques: Recherches sur les migrations des contes populaires*. Paris: Champion.

1922. Genzel, Adolf. "Die Helfer und Schädiger des Helden im deutschen Volksmärchen." Diss. University of Leipzig.

1922. Heyden, Franz. *Volksmärchen und Volksmärchenerzähler: Zur literarischen Gestaltung des deutschen Volksmärchens*. Hamburg: Hanseatische Verlagsanstalt.

1922. Naumann, Hans. *Grundzüge der deutschen Volkskunde*. Wissenschaft und Bildung, 181. Leipzig: Quelle & Meyer.

1922. Tegethoff, Ernst. *Studien zum Märchentypus von Amor und Psyche*. Diss. University of Munich 1922. Rheinische Beiträge und Hülfsbücher zur germanischen Philologie und Volkskunde, 4. Bonn and Leipzig: Schroeder.

1923. Huet, Gédéon. *Les contes populaires*. Paris: Flammarion.

1923. Philippson, Ernst Alfred. *Der Märchentypus vom König Drosselbart*. Diss. University of Cologne 1922. FFC, 50. Greifswald: Suomalainen Tiedeakatemia / Academia scientificarum fennica.

1923. Saintyves, Pierre (pseud. for Émile Nourry). *Les contes de Perrault et les récits parallèles: Leurs origines (coutumes primitives et liturgies populaires)*. Paris: Nourry.

1924. Wisser, Wilhelm. "Das Märchen von einem, der auszog, das Fürchten zu lernen." *Nordelbingen: Beiträge zur Heimatforschung in Schleswig-Holstein, Hamburg und Lübeck* 3: 63-76.

1925. Bülow, Werner von. *Die Geheimsprache der deutschen Märchen: Ein Beitrag zur Entwickelungsgeschichte der deutschen Religion*. Hellerau bei Dresden: Hakenkreuz.

1925. Wesselski, Albert. *Märchen des Mittelalters*. Berlin: Stubenrauch.

1925. Wisser, Wilhelm. *Das Märchen im Volksmund: Dumm Hans mit der Königstochter im Elternhaus. Im Anhang: Das Märchen vom Drachentöter.* Hamburg: Quickborn.

1927-42. Bächtold-Stäubli, Hanns, ed. *Handwörterbuch des deutschen Aberglaubens.* 10 vols. Berlin and Leipzig: de Gruyter.

1928. de Boor, Helmut. "Märchenforschung." In Karlinger, ed. 1973, 129-54. Reprint from *Zeitschrift für den deutschen Unterricht* 42: 561-81.

1928. Müller, Erwin. *Psychologie des deutschen Volksmärchens.* Diss. University of Würzburg 1927. Munich: Kösel & Pustet.

1928. Propp, Vladimir. *Morfologija skazki.* Voprosy poetiki, 12. Leningrad: Academia. Translated into English as *Morphology of the Folktale.* Trans. Laurence Scott. 2nd rev. ed. Ed. Louis A. Wagner. Publications of the American Folklore Society: Bibliographical & Special Series, 9; Indiana University Research Center in Anthropology, Folklore, and Linguistics, 10. Austin: University of Texas Press, 1968.

1928. Rösch, Erich. *Der getreue Johannes: Eine vergleichende Märchenstudie.* Rev. Diss. University of Heidelberg 1925. FFC, 77. Helsinki: Suomalainen Tiedeakatemia/ Academia scientificarum fennica.

1928. Storer, Mary Elizabeth. *Un episode littéraire de la fin du xviie siècle: La mode des contes des fées.* Bibliothèque de la Revue de la littérature comparée, 48. Paris: Champion.

1928. Thompson, Stith. *The Types of the Folktale: A Classification and Bibliography.* FFC, 74. Helsinki: Suomalainen Tiedeakatemia / Academia scientificarum fennica. (A translation, revision, and enlargement of Aarne 1910.) 2nd ed. FFC, 184. Helsinki: Suomalainen Tiedeakatemia / Academia scientificarum fennica, 1961.

1928. Winterstein, Alfred. "Die Pubertätsriten der Mädchen und ihre Spuren im Märchen." *Imago* 14: 199-274. Partially reprinted in Laiblin, ed. 1969, 56-70.

1929. de Vries, Jan. *Het Sprookje: Opstellen..* Antwerp, etc.: Standaard-Boekhandel, n.d.

1929. Freitag, Elisabeth. *Die KHM der Brüder Grimm im ersten Stadium ihrer stilgeschichtlichen Entwicklung: Vergleich der Urform (Oelenberger Hs.) mit dem Erstdruck von 1812.* Diss. University of Frankfurt am Main 1929. Oestrich im Reingau: Etienne.

1929. Haavio, Martti. *Kettenmärchenstudien.* Diss. University of Helsinki 1929. FFC, 88. Helsinki: Suomalainen Tiedeakatemia/Academia Scientificarum fennica.

1930. Heckmann, Emil. *Blaubart: Ein Beitrag zur vergleichenden Märchenforschung.* Diss. University of Heidelberg 1930. n.p.: n.p.

1930. Jolles, André. *Einfache Formen: Legende, Sage, Mythe, Rätsel, Spruch, Kasus, Memorabile, Märchen, Witz.* Halle: Niemeyer. 5th ed. ("Studienausgabe der 4. Auflage") Tübingen: Niemeyer, 1972. Also in the series Konzepte der Sprach- und Literaturwissenschaft, 15. Tübingen: Niemeyer, 1982.

1930. Krappe, Alexander Haggerty. *The Science of Folk-Lore*. London: Methuen.

1930-40. Mackensen, Lutz, ed. *Handwörterbuch des deutschen Märchens*. 2 vols. Handwörterbücher zur deutschen Volkskunde, Abteilung II: Märchen. Berlin and Leipzig: de Gruyter.

1930. Müller, Erwin. "Traum und Märchenphantasie." *Zeitschrift für pädagogische Psychologie* 31: 72-84. Reprint in Laiblin, ed. 1969, 71-87.

1930. Schoof, Wilhelm. "Zur Entstehungsgeschichte der Grimmschen Märchen." *Hessische Blätter für Volkskunde* 29:1-118. See also Schoof. 1959.

1930. Velten, H. V. "The Influence of Charles Perrault's *Contes de ma mère l'oie* on German Folklore." *The Germanic Review* 5: 4-18.

1931. Honti, Hans. *Volksmärchen und Heldensage: Beiträge zur Klärung ihrer Zusammenhänge*. FFC, 95. Helsinki: Suomalainen Tiedeakatemia / Academia scientificarum fennica.

1931. Krohn, Kaarle. *Übersicht über einige Resultate der Märchenforschung*. FFC, 96. Helsinki: Suomalainen Tiedeakatemia / Academia scientificarum fennica.

1931. Wesselski, Albert. *Versuch einer Theorie des Märchens*. Prager deutsche Studien, 45. Reichenberg (Bohemia): Sudetendeutscher Verlag Franz Kraus.

1932. Giese, Wilhelm. "Zur Morphologie der Märchen der Romanen." In Anon., ed. *Miscellanea Filologica dedicada a D. Antonio Alcover*. Palma de Mallorca: Piza.

1932. Rosenbaum, Marie-Elisabeth. *Liebe und Ehe im deutschen Volksmärchen*. Diss. University of Jena 1929. Klosterlausnitz: n. p.

1932. Schmidt, Kurt. *Die Entwicklung der Grimmschen Kinder- und Hausmärchen seit der Urhandschrift: Nebst einem kritischen Texte der in die Drucke übergegangenen Stücke*. Diss. University of Halle 1931. Hermaea, 30. Halle: Niemeyer.

1932. Schulte-Kemminghausen, Karl. *Die niederdeutschen Märchen der Brüder Grimm*. Veröffentlichungen der volkskundlichen Kommission des Provinzialinstituts für westfälische Landes- und Volkskunde: Dritte Reihe, 1. Münster in Westfalen: Aschendorff.

1932-36. Thompson, Stith. *Motif-Index of Folk-Literature: A Classification of Narrative Elements in Folktale, Ballads, Myths, Fables, Medieval Romances, Exempla, Jest Books and Local Legends*. 6 vols. FFC, 106-109. Copenhagen: Rosenkilde and Bagger. 2nd ed. 1955-58.

1933. Bornstein, Steff. "Das Märchen von Dornröschen in psychoanalytischer Darstellung." *Imago* 19: 505-17.

1933. Romain, Alfred. "Zur Gestalt des Grimmschen Dornröschen Märchens." *Zeitschrift für Volkskunde* 42 [=n.s. 4]: 84-116.

1933. Wesselski, Albert. "Das Märlein von dem Tode des Hühnchens [*KHM* 80] und andere Kettenmärlein." *Hessische Blätter für Volkskunde* 32:1-51.

1934. Duff, J. F. Grant. "Schneewittchen: Versuch einer psychoanalytischen Deutung." *Imago* 20: 95-103. Reprint in Laiblin, ed. 1969, 88-99.

1934. Ranke, Kurt. *Die zwei Brüder: Eine Studie zur vergleichenden Märchenforschung.* FFC, 114. Helsinki: Suomalainen Tiedeakatemia/ Academica scientificarum fennica.

1935. Anderson, Walter. *Zu Albert Wesselski's Angriffen auf die finnische folkloristische Forschungsmethode.* Eesti Rahvaluule Arhiivi Toimetsued / Commentationes archivi traditionum popularum estoniae, 4. Tartu: K. Matthiesen.

1935. Meyer, Rudolf. *Die Weisheit der deutschen Volksmärchen.* Stuttgart: Christengemeinschaft. 3rd ed. Stuttgart: Urachhaus, 1954. 6th ed. 1969.

1936. Laiblin, Wilhelm. "Das Urbild der Mutter." *Zentralblatt für Psychotherapie und ihre Grenzgebiete einschließlich der medizinischen Psychologie und psychischen Hygiene* 9, nos. 2-3. Partial reprint in Laiblin, ed. 1969, 100-50.

1936. Ranke, Friedrich. "Märchenforschung: Ein Literaturbericht (1920-1934)." *Deutsche Vierteljahrsschrift für Literaturwissenschaft und Geistesgeschichte* 14: 246-304.

1937. Jürgens, Wilhelm. *Der Wirklichkeitsgehalt des Märchens: Untersuchungen zur Ontologie des mythischen Bewußtseins.* Diss. University of Kiel 1937. Kiel: Schmidt & Klaunig.

1937. Tönges, Konrad. *Lebenserscheinungen und Verbreitung des deutschen Märchens.* Gießener Beiträge zur deutschen Philologie, 56. Gießen: von Münchow.

1938. Herzog, Jozef. *Die Märchentypen des 'Ritter Blaubart' und 'Fitchervogel'.* Würzburg: Konrad Triltsch.

1938. Peuckert, Will-Erich. *Deutsches Volkstum in Märchen und Sage, Schwank und Rätsel.* Deutsches Volkstum, 2. Berlin: de Gruyter.

1938. Prestel, Josef. *Märchen als Lebensdichtung: Das Werk der Brüder Grimm.* Munich: Hueber.

1938. Wesselski, Albert. *Deutsche Märchen vor Grimm.* Brünn and Leipzig: Rohrer.

1939. Jöckel, Bruno. *Der Weg zum Märchen.* Berlin-Stieglitz: Dion-Verlag Liebmann & Mette.

1939. Spanner, Werner. *Das Märchen als Gattung.* Gießener Beiträge zur deutschen Philologie, 68. Gießen: von Münchow. Partial reprint in Karlinger, ed. 1973, 155-76.

1940. Mehlem, Richard. "Niederdeutsche Quellen der Grimmschen KHM unter besonderer Berücksichtigung Niedersachsens." *Archiv für Landes- und Volkskunde in Niedersachsen* 1: 49-99.

1941. Schoof, Wilhelm. "Schneewittchen: Ein Beitrag zur deutschen Stilkunde." *Germanisch-Romanische Monatsschrift* 29: 190-201.

1943. Bilz, Josephine. *Menschliche Reifung im Sinnbild: Eine psychologische Untersuchung über Wandlungsmetaphern des Traums, des Wahns und des Märchens.* Zentralblatt für Psychotherapie, supps. 5. Leipzig: Hirzel. Partial reprint in Laiblin, ed. 1969, 161-86.

1943. Laiblin, Wilhelm. "Die Symbolik der Erlösung und Wiedergeburt im deutschen Volksmärchen." *Zentralblatt für Psychotherapie und ihre Grenzgebiete, einschließlich der medizinischen Psychologie und psychischen Hygiene* 15: 93-129.

1943. Lüthi, Max. *Die Gabe im Märchen und in der Sage: Ein Beitrag zur Wesenserfassung und Wesensscheidung der beiden Formen.* Diss. University of Berne. Berne: Büchler.

1945. Koechlin, Elisabeth. *Wesenszüge des deutschen und des französischen Volksmärchens: Eine vergleichende Studie zum Märchentypus von "Amor und Psyche" und vom "Tierbräutigam".* Basler Studien zur Deutschen Sprache und Literatur, 4. Basel: Schwabe.

1945. Philippson, Ernst Alfred. "Um Grundsätzliches in der Märchenforschung." *Monatshefte für den deutschen Unterricht* 37, 4-5 (April/May; "M. Blakemore Evans Number"): 135-50.

1946/47; 1952. Anon. "Märchen-Bibliographie: Seit 1945 erschienen im Gebiet der Deutschen Demokratischen Republik." *Der Bibliothekar: Monatsschrift für das Bibliothekswesen* 1-3; 6: 449-52.

1946. Propp, Vladimir. *Istoricheskie korni volshebnoi skazki.* Leningrad: Lenin University. Translated by Lise Gruel-Apert as *Les Racines historiques du conte merveilleux.* Paris: Gallimard, 1983. Translated by Martin Pfeiffer as *Die historischen Wurzeln des Zaubermärchens.* Munich and Vienna: Hanser, 1987.

1946. Thompson, Stith. *The Folktale.* Reprint Berkeley: University of California Press, 1977.

1947. Kiefer, Emma Emily. *Albert Wesselski and Recent Folktale Theories.* Indiana University Publications: Folklore Series, 3. Bloomington: Indiana University.

1947. Lüthi, Max. *Das europäische Volksmärchen: Form und Wesen. Eine literaturwissenschaftliche Darstellung.* Dalp-Taschenbücher, 351. 2nd exp. and rev. ed. Berne and Munich: Francke, 1960. 3rd exp. ed. 1968. 4th exp. ed. 1974. Also 1981. Translated by John D. Niles as *The European Folktale: Form and Nature.* Philadelphia: Institute for the Study of Human Issues, 1982.

1948. Jöckel, Bruno. "Das Reifungserlebnis im Märchen." *Psyche* 1, no. 3: 382-95. Partial reprint in Laiblin, ed. 1969, 195-211.

1948a. Sydow, Carl Wilhelm von. *Selected Papers on Folklore: Published on the Occasion of His 70th Birthday.* Copenhagen: Rosenkilde and Bagger.

1948b. Sydow, Carl Wilhelm von. "Märchenforschung und Philologie." In Karlinger, ed. 1973, 177-93. Reprinted from *Universitas* 3: 1047-58.

1949. Campbell, Joseph. *The Hero with a Thousand Faces.* Bollingen Series, 17. New York: Pantheon. Reprint New York: Meridian, 1956.

1949. Ernst, Fritz. *Dornröschen in drei Sprachen.* Berne: Hans Huber. Reprint in Fritz Ernst. *Aus Goethes Freundeskreis und andere Essays.* Frankfurt a.m.: Suhrkamp. 1955, 135-60.

1949. Leach, Maria, ed. *Funk & Wagnalls Standard Dictionary of Folklore, Mythology and Legend.* 2 vols. New York: Funk and Wagnalls.

1949. Loeffler-Delachaux, Marguerite. *Le Symbolisme des contes des fées.* Paris: L'Arche.

1950/51. Delarue, Paul. "Les Contes merveilleux de Perrault et la tradition populaire: Introduction." *Bulletin folklorique d'Île-de-France,* n.s. 12: 195-201.

1950/51. Delarue, Paul. "Les Contes merveilleux de Perrault et la tradition populaire: I. Le petit Chaperon rouge." *Bulletin folklorique d'Ile-de-France* n.s. 12: 221-28, 251-60, 283-91.

1951. Anderson, Walter. *Ein volkskundliches Experiment.* FFC, 141. Helsinki: Suomalainen Tiedeakatemia / Academia scientificarum fennica.

1951. Dymke, Anneliese. "Die wirkliche Welt im deutschen Zaubermärchen: Studien zum Märchengepräge." Diss. University of Würzburg.

1951. Fromm, Erich. *The Forgotten Language: An Introduction to the Understanding of Dreams, Fairy Tales and Myths.* New York: Rinehart. Translated into German as *Märchen, Mythen und Träume: Eine Einführung zum Verständnis von Träumen, Märchen und Mythen.* Trans. Ernst Bucher. Zurich: Diana, 1957.

1951. Hendricks, Hildegard. "Die beseelten Tiergestalten des deutschen Volksmärchens und ihre Entsprechung im Volksglauben." Diss. University of Bonn.

1951. Rooth, Anna Birgitta. *The Cinderella Cycle.* Diss. University of Lund 1951. Lund: Gleerup. Reprint New York: Arno, 1980.

1951. Rumpf, Marianne. "Rotkäppchen: Eine vergleichende Untersuchung." Diss. University of Göttingen.

1952-57. Beit, Hedwig [Roques-] von. *Symbolik des Märchens: Versuch einer Deutung.* 3 vols. Berne: Francke. 2nd ed. 1960.

1952. Delarue, Paul. "Les Contes merveilleux de Perrault et la tradition populaire: II. Barbe-bleue." *Bulletin folklorique d'Île-de-France,* n.s. 13: 348-57.

1952. Neumann, Erich, ed. *Apuleius Madaurensis. Amor und Psyche. Mit einem Kommentar von Erich Neumann. Ein Beitrag zur seelischen Entwicklung des Weiblichen.* Zurich: Rascher [1951]. Translated by Ralph Manheim as *Amor und Psyche: The Psychic Development of the Feminine. A Commentary of the Tale by Apuleius.* Bollinger Series, 54. New York: Pantheon.

1952. Seifert-Korschinek, Edeltraud. "Untersuchungen zu Grimms Märchen 'Das Marienkind.'" Diss. University of Munich.

1953. Hartmann-Ströhm, Ingrid. "'Das Meerhäschen': Eine vergleichende Märchenuntersuchung." Diss. University of Göttingen.

1953. Röhrich, Lutz. "Mensch und Tier im Märchen." *Schweizerisches Archiv für Volkskunde* 49: 165-93. Reprinted in Karlinger, ed. 1973, 220-53.

1953. Schoof, Wilhelm. "Neue Urfassungen Grimmscher Märchen." *Hessische Blätter für Volkskunde* 44: 65-88.

1954. Cocchiara, Giuseppe. *Storia del Folklore in Europa.* Colezione di studi religiosi, etnologici e psicologici, 20. Turin: Einaudi.

1954. de Vries, Jan. 1954. *Betrachtungen zum Märchen: Besonders in seinem Verhältnis zu Heldensage und Mythos.* FFC, 150. Helsinki: Suomalainen Tiedeakatemia / Academia scientificarum fennica.

1954. Delarue, Paul. "Les contes merveilleux de Perrault: Faits et rapprochements nouveaux." *Arts et traditions populaires: Revue trimestrielle de la Société d'Ethnographie Française* 2: 1-22, 251-74.

1954. Hagen, Rolf. "Der Einfluß der Perraultschen Contes auf das volkstümliche deutsche Erzählgut und besonders auf die Kinder- und Hausmärchen der Brüder Grimm." 2 vols. Diss. University of Göttingen 1954.

1954. Ussher, Arland, and Carl von Metzradt. *Enter These Enchanted Woods: An Interpretation of Grimm's Fairy Tales.* 2nd ed. Introd. Padraic Colum. Chester Springs, PA: Dufour, 1966.

1955. Bausinger, Hermann. "'Aschenputtel': Zum Problem der Märchensymbolik." *Zeitschrift für Volkskunde* 52: 144-55. Reprint in Laiblin, ed. 1969, 284-98.

1955. Franz, Marie Luise von. "Bei der schwarzen Frau: Deutungsversuch eines Märchens." In *Studien zur analytischen Psychologie C. G. Jungs.* Vol. 2: *Beiträge zur Kulturgeschichte.* Zürich: Rascher. 1-41. Reprint in Laiblin, ed. 1969, 299-344.

1955. Hagen, Rolf. "Perraults Märchen und die Brüder Grimm." *Zeitschrift für Deutsche Philologie* 74: 392-410.

1955. Leber, Gabriele. "Über tiefenpsychologische Aspekte von Märchenmotiven." *Praxis der Kinderpsychologie und Kinderpsychiatrie* 4: 274-85.

1955. Lévi-Strauss, Claude. "The Structural Study of Myth." *Journal of American Folklore* 68: 428-44.

1955. Pinon, Roger. *Le Conte merveilleux comme sujet d'Études.* Liège: Centre d'Education Populaire et de Culture.

1955-57. Röhrich, Lutz. "Die Märchenforschung seit dem Jahre 1945." *Deutsches Jahrbuch für Volkskunde* (Berlin [East]) 1: 279-96, 2: 274-319, 3: 213-24, 494-514.

1955. Rumpf, Marianne. *Ursprung und Entstehung von Warn- und Schreckmärchen.* FFC, 160. Helsinki: Suomalainen Tiedeakatemia/ Academia scientificarum fennica.

1955. Schier, Kurt. *Praktische Untersuchungen zur mündlichen Wiedergabe von Volkserzählungen.* Diss. University of Munich 1955. Munich: Omnia (Krauss, Weiss und Co.).

1955. Schoof, Wilhelm. "Beiträge zur Stilentwicklung der Grimmschen Märchen." *Zeitschrft für Deutsche Philologie* 74: 424-33.

1955. Swahn, Jan-Öjvind. *The Tale of Cupid and Psyche (Aarne-Thompson 425 & 428)*. Lund: Gleerup.

1955. Thompson, Stith. *Narrative Motif-Analysis as a Folklore Method*. FFC, 161. Helsinki: Suomalainen Tiedeakatemia / Academia scientificarum fennica.

1956. Anderson, Walter. *Eine neue Arbeit zur experimentellen Volkskunde*. FFC, 168. Helsinki: Suomalainen Tiedeakatemia / Academia scientificarum fennica.

1956. Eliade, Mircea. "Wissenschaft und Märchen." In Karlinger, ed. 1973, 311-19. Translation of "Les savants et les contes de fées." *Nouvelle Revue française* 3: 884-91.

1956. Handschin-Ninck. "Ältester und Jüngster im Märchen." *Praxis der Kinderpsychologie und Kinderpsychiatrie* 5: 167-73.

1956. Laiblin, Wilhelm. "Symbolik der Wandlung im Märchen." In Wilhelm Bitter, ed. *Die Wandlung des Menschen in Seelsorge und Psychotherapie*. Göttingen: Verlag für Medizinische Psychologie. 276-300. Reprint in Laiblin, ed. 1969, 345-74.

1956. Lüthi, Max. "Das Volksmärchen als Dichtung und als Aussage." *Der Deutschunterricht* no. 6: 5-17. Reprint in Karlinger, ed. 1973, 295-310.

1956a. Röhrich, Lutz. *Märchen und Wirklichkeit: Eine volkskundliche Untersuchung*. Wiesbaden: Franz Steiner. 4th ed. 1979.

1956b. Röhrich, Lutz. "Neue Wege der Märchenforschung." *Der Deutschunterricht* 8, no. 6: 92-116.

1956/57. Schoof, Wilhelm. "Der Froschkönig oder der eiserne Heinrich: Ein Beitrag zur Stilentwicklung der Grimmschen Märchen." *Wirkendes Wort* 7: 45-49.

1957. D'Aronco, Gianfranco. *Le fiabe di magia in Italia*. Udine: Arti Grafiche Friulane.

1957/1964. Delarue, Paul, and Marie-Louise Tenèze. *Le Conte populaire français: Catalogue raisonné des versions de France et des pays de langue français d'outre-mer [...]*. 2 vols. Paris: Maisonneuve et Lavose. 2nd ed. 1976/1977.

1957/58. Kalho, Gerhard. "Frau Holle und der Nobiskrug." *Wissenschaftliche Beiträge der Friedrich-Schiller-Universität Jena: Gesellschafts- und sprachwissenschaftliche Reihe* 7: 583-89.

1958. Bühler, Charlotte, and Josephine Bilz. *Das Märchen und die Phantasie des Kindes*. 2nd ed. Munich: Barth, 1961.

1958. de Vries, Jan. "Dornröschen." *Fabula* 2:110-21.

1958. Lüthi, Max. *Rapunzel*. Kommentare zum Schweizerischen Schulwandbilderwerk, 98. Zurich: Schweizerischer Lehrerverein.

1958. Ranke, Kurt. "Betrachtungen zum Wesen und zur Funktion des Märchens." *Studium Generale* 11: 647-64. Reprint in Karlinger, ed. 1973, 320-60.

1958. Roberts, Warren. *The Tale of the Kind and the Unkind Girls: AA-TH 480 and Related Tales*. Rev. diss. Indiana University 1953. *Fabula* supps.: Reihe B - Untersuchungen, 1. Berlin: de Gruyter.

1958. Wolfersdorf, Peter. *Märchen und Sage in Forschung, Schule und Jugendpflege*. Braunschweig: Waisenhaus.

1959. Lüthi, Max. "Rapunzel." In Max Lüthi. *Volksmärchen und Volkssage: Zwei Grundformen erzählender Dichtung*. Berne and Munich: Francke, 1961, 62-96. 3rd ed. 1975. Originally as "Die Herkunft des Grimmschen Rapunzelmärchens (AaTh 310)." *Fabula* 3: 95-118.

1959. Obenauer, Karl Justus. *Das Märchen: Dichtung und Deutung*. Frankfurt am Main: Vittorio Klostermann.

1959. Schoof, Wilhelm. *Zur Entstehungsgeschichte der Grimmschen Märchen: Bearbeitet unter Benutzung des Nachlasses der Brüder Grimm*. Hamburg: Hauswedell.

1959. Uhlrich, Herta. "Volksdichtung: Eine Übersicht über Veröffentlichungen aus den Jahren 1956 bis 1959." *Deutsches Jahrbuch für Volkskunde* (Berlin-East) 5: 183-202.

1961. Birkhan, Helmut. "Die Verwandlung in der Volkserzählung: Eine Untersuchung zur Phänomenologie der Verwandlungssymbolik mit besonderer Berücksichtigung der Märchen der Brüder Grimm." Diss. University of Vienna.

1961-62. Jobes, Gertrude. *Dictionary of Mythology, Folklore and Symbols*. 3 vols. New York: Scarecrow.

1961. Klöne, Ursula. *Die Aufnahme des Märchens in der italienischen Kunstprosa von Straparola bis Basile*. Diss. University of Marburg 1961. Marburg: Mauersberger.

1961. Liungman, Waldemar. *Die schwedischen Volksmärchen: Herkunft und Geschichte*. Deutsche Akademie der Wissenschaften zu Berlin: Veröffentlichungen des Instituts für Deutsche Volkskunde, 20. Berlin: Akademie Verlag.

1961. Mendelsohn, J. "Das Tiermärchen und seine Bedeutung als Ausdruck seelischer Entwicklungsstruktur: Teil I." *Praxis der Kinderpsychologie und Kinderpsychiatrie* 10: 8-13.

1962. Dégh, Linda. *Märchen, Erzähler und Erzählgemeinschaft: Dargestellt an der ungarischen Volksüberlieferung*. Berlin (East): Akademie-Verlag.

1962a. Lüthi, Max. *Märchen*. Sammlung Metzler, 16. Stuttgart: Metzler. 2nd rev. ed. 1964. 8th rev. and exp ed. Ed. Heinz Rölleke. 1990.

1962b. Lüthi, Max. "Dornröschen: Vom Sinn und Gewand des Märchens." In Max Lüthi. *Es war einmal [...]: Vom Wesen des Volksmärchens*. Kleine Vandenhoeck Reihe, 136/137. Göttingen: Vandenhoeck & Ruprecht. 5-18.

1962/1967. Röhrich, Lutz. *Erzählungen des späten Mittelalters und ihr Weiterleben in Literatur und Volksdichtung bis zur Gegenwart: Sagen, Märchen, Exempel und Schwänke mit einem Kommentar*. 2 vols. Berne and Munich: Francke.

1962. Rougemont, Charlotte. *[...] dann leben sie noch heute: Erlebnisse und Erfahrungen beim Märchenerzählen.* Schriften der Gesellschaft zur Pflege des Märchengutes der europäischen Völker, 1. Münster: Aschendorff. 6th ed. 1977.

1962. Winter, Elisabeth. "Ur- und Endfassung des Grimmschen Märchens 'Hänsel und Gretel.'" *Pädagogische Rundschau* 16: 808-19.

1963. Barchilon, Jacques. "Uses of the Fairy Tale in the Eighteenth Century." *Studies on Voltaire and the Eighteenth Century* 24: 111-38.

1963. Bittner, Günther. "Über die Symbolik weiblicher Reifung im Märchen." *Praxis der Kinderpsychologie und Kinderpsychiatrie* 12: 210-13. Reprint in Laiblin, ed. 1969, 410-17.

1963. Freudmann, Felix R. "Realism and Magic in Perrault's Fairy Tales." *L'Esprit créateur* 3: 116-22.

1963. Ginschel, Gunhild. "Der Märchenstil Jacob Grimms." *Deutsches Jahrbuch für Volkskunde* (Berlin [East]) 9: 131-68.

1963. Heuscher, Julius E. *A Psychiatric Study of Fairy Tales.* Springfield, IL: Thomas. 2nd rev. and enl. ed., titled *A Psychiatric Study of Myths and Fairy Tales: Their Origin, Meaning and Usefulness.* 1974.

1963. Karlinger, Felix. "Schneeweißchen und Rosenrot in Sardinien: Zur Übernahme eines Buchmärchens in die volkstümliche Tradition." In Ludwig Denecke and Ina-Maria Greverus, eds. *Brüder Grimm Gedenken 1963.* Marburg: Elwert. 585-93.

1963. Schmidt, Leopold. *Die Volkserzählung: Märchen, Sage, Legende, Schwank.* Berlin: Erich Schmidt.

1963. Schoof, Wilhelm. "Zur Geschichte des Grimmschen Märchenstils." *Der Deutschunterricht* 15, no. 2 (June): 90-99.

1963. Traxler, Hans. *Die Wahrheit über Hänsel und Gretel: Eine Dokumentation des Märchens der Brüder Grimm.* Frankfurt am Main: Bärmeier und Nikel.

1963. Zillinger, G. "Zur Frage der Angst und der Darstellung psychosexueller Reifungsstufen im 'Märchen vom Gruseln': Eine analytische Studie." *Praxis der Kinderpsychologie und Kinderpsychiatrie* 12: 33-41, 107-12, 134-43.

1964. David, Alfred, and Mary Elizabeth David. "A Literary Approach to the Brothers Grimm." *Journal of the Folklore Institute* (Indiana University) 1:180-96.

1964. Fink, Gonthier-Louis. "Les avatars de Rumpelstilzchen: La Vie d'un Conte Populaire." In Ernst Kracht, ed. *Deutsch-französische Gespräche im Lichte der Märchen.* Schriften der Gesellschaft zur Pflege des Märchengutes der europäischen Völker, 2. Münster: Aschendorff. 46-72.

1964. Getto, Giovanni. "Il barocco et la fiaba di Giambattista Basile." In *Linguistic and Literary Studies in Honor of Helmut A. Hatzfeld.* Ed. Alessandro S. Crisafulli. Washington, DC: Catholic University of America Press. 185-201.

1964. Lo Nigro, Sebastiano. *Tradizione e invenzione nel racconto popolare.* Istituto di Storia delle Tradizioni Popolari dell'Università di Catania, 2. Florence: Olschki. Partial German translation in Karlinger, ed. 1973, 372-93.

1965. Mallet, Carl-Heinz. "Die zweite und dritte Nacht im Märchen 'Das Gruseln.'" *Praxis der Kinderpsychologie und Kinderpsychiatrie* 14 (1965): 216-20.

1965. Stumpfe, Ortrud. *Die Symbolsprache der Märchen.* Schriften der Gesellschaft zur Pflege des Märchengutes der europäischen Völker, 3. 3rd ed. Münster: Aschendorff, 1975.

1965. Wittgenstein, Ottokar Graf. *Märchen, Träume, Schicksale.* Düsseldorf and Cologne: Diederichs.

1966. Dieckmann, Hans. *Märchen und Träume als Helfer der Menschen.* Stuttgart: Bonz. 2nd ed., titled *Märchen und Symbole: Tiefenpsychologische Deutung orientalischer Märchen.* Psychologisch gesehen, 4. Stuttgart: Bonz, 1968.

1966. Fink, Gonthier-Louis. *Naissance et apogée du conte merveilleux en Allemagne 1740-1800.* Annales littéraires de l'Université de Besançon, 80. Paris: Les Belles Lettres.

1966/67. Kahn, Otto. "Rumpelstilz hat wirklich gelebt: Textvergleichende Studie über das Märchen vom Rumpelstilzchen (AaTh 500) und eine Erklärung mit Hilfe der Rechtsgeschichte. Ein Versuch." *Rheinisches Jahrbuch für Volkskunde* 17/18: 143-84.

1966. Veszy-Wagner, Lilla. "Little Red Riding Hood on the Couch." *The Psychoanalytic Forum* 1: 400-08.

1967. Barchilon, Jacques. "L'ironie et l'humour dans les 'Contes' de Perrault." *Studi francese* 11: 258-70.

1967. Gehrts, Heino. *Das Märchen und das Opfer: Untersuchungen zum europäischen Brüdermärchen.* Bonn: Bouvier.

1967. Ginschel, Gunhild. "Aufzeichnung und Bearbeitung der Kinder- und Hausmärchen." In Gunhild Ginschel. *Der junge Jacob Grimm: 1805-1819.* Deutsche Akademie der Wissenschaften zu Berlin: Veröffentlichungen der Sprachwissenschaftlichen Kommission zu Berlin, 7. Berlin (East): Akademie Verlag, 212-78.

1967. Robert, Marthe. "The Grimm Brothers." Trans. Wylie L. Powell. In Peter Brooks, ed. *The Child's Part.* Yale French Studies, 43. New Haven: Yale French Studies, 44-56. Originally as "Les Frères Grimm," in Marthe Robert, *Sur le Papier.* Paris: Grasset, 1967.

1967. Röhrich, Lutz. "Zwölfmal Rotkäppchen." In Lutz Röhrich. *Gebärde, Metapher, Parodie: Studien zur Sprache und Volksdichtung. Wirkendes Wort:* Schriftenreihe, 4. Düsseldorf: Pädagogischer Verlag Schwann. 130-52.

1967. Sandford, Beryl. "Cinderella." *The Psychoanalytic Forum* 2: 128-32.

1968. Bausinger, Hermann. *Formen der 'Volkspoesie'.* Grundlagen der Germanistik, 6. Berlin: Erich Schmidt. 2nd enl. & rev. ed. 1980.

1968. Federspiel, Christa. *Vom Volksmärchen zum Kindermärchen*. Diss. University of Vienna 1966. Dissertationen der Universität Wien, 4. Vienna: Notring.

1968. Gutter, Agnes. *Märchen und Märe: Psychologische Deutung und pädagogische Wertung*. Arbeiten zur Psychologie, Pädagogik und Heilpädagogik, 24. Solothurn (Switzerland): Antonius-Verlag.

1968a. Soriano, Marc. *Les Contes de Perrault: Culture savante et traditions populaires*. Paris: Gallimard. 2nd ed. 1977.

1968b. Soriano, Marc. "Le petit chaperon rouge." *La Nouvelle Revue Française* 16: 429-43.

1969. Cook, Elizabeth. *The Ordinary and the Fabulous: An Introduction to Myths, Legends, and Fairy Tales for Teachers and Storytellers*. Cambridge: Cambridge University Press.

1969. Karlinger, Felix. *Einführung in die romanische Volksliteratur. 1. Teil: Die romanische Volksprosa*. Munich: Hueber.

1969. Laiblin, Wilhelm, ed. *Märchenforschung und Tiefenpsychologie*. Wege der Forschung, 102. Darmstadt: Wissenschaftliche Buchgesellschaft.

1969. Lüthi, Max. *So leben sie heute noch: Betrachtungen zum Volksmärchen*. Kleine Vandenhoeck-Reihe, 294-96. Göttingen: Vandenhoeck & Ruprecht.

1970/1971. Briggs, Katherine M. *A Dictionary of British Folk-Tales in the English Language, Incorporating the F. J. Norton Collection*. 2 vols. in 4. Bloomington: Indiana University Press.

1970. Franz, Marie-Louise von. *An Introduction to the Psychology of Fairy Tales*. 2nd ed. New York and Zurich: Spring Publications, 1973. Original title *An Introduction to the Interpretation of Fairy Tales*.

1970. Giehrl, Hans Eberhard. *Volksmärchen und Tiefenpsychologie*. Schriften der pädagogischen Hochschulen Bayerns. Munich: Ehrenwerth.

1970. Londeix, Georges. *Le petit chaperon rouge de Perrault*. Paris: L'Herne.

1970. Weber-Kellermann, Ingeborg. "Interethnische Gedanken beim Lesen der Grimmschen Märchen." *Acta Ethnographica Academiae Scientiarum Hungaricae* (Budapest) 19: 425-34.

1971. Lenz, Friedel. *Bildsprache der Märchen*. Stuttgart: Urachhaus. 3rd ed. 1976.

1971. Lüthi, Max. "Rumpelstilzchen: Thematik, Struktur und Stiltendenzen innerhalb eines Märchentypus." *Antaios* 12: 419-36.

1971. Michaelis-Jena, Ruth. "Oral Tradition and the Brothers Grimm." *Folklore* 82: 265-75.

1972. Burns, Lee. "Red Riding Hood." *Children's Literature* 1: 30-36.

1972. Franz, Marie-Louise von. *Problems of the Feminine in Fairy Tales*. Zurich: Spring Publications. Rev. ed. New York: Spring Publications, 1976.

1972/73. Lieberman, Marcia R. "'Some Day My Prince Will Come': Female Acculturation through the Fairy Tale." *College English* 34: 383-95.

1972. Mönckeberg[-Kolmar], Vilma. *Das Märchen und unsere Welt: Erfahrungen und Einsichten.* Düsseldorf and Cologne: Diederichs.

1972/73. Röhrich, Lutz. "Rumpelstilzchen: Vom Methodenpluralismus in der Erzählforschung." In Röhrich. 1976, 272-91. Originally *Schweizerisches Archiv für Volkskunde* 68/69: 567-96.

1972. Rölleke, Heinz. "Allerleirauh: Eine bisher unbekannte Fassung vor Grimm." *Fabula* 13:153-59. Reprinted in Rölleke. 1985, 175-83.

1973. Karlinger, Felix, ed. *Wege der Märchenforschung.* Wege der Forschung, 255. Darmstadt: Wissenschaftliche Buchgesellschaft.

1973. Pongs, Hermann. "Symbolsprache der Grimmschen Märchen." In Hermann Pongs. *Das Bild in der Dichtung.* Vol. 4: *Symbolik der einfachen Formen.* Marburg: Elwert, 44-118.

1973. Rölleke, Heinz. "Von dem Fischer und syner Fru: Die älteste schriftliche Überlieferung." *Fabula* 14: 112-23. Reprinted in Rölleke. 1985, 161-74.

1974. Franz, Marie-Louise von. *Shadow and Evil in Fairy Tales.* New York and Zurich: Spring Publications.

1974. Jäger, Hans-Wolf. "Trägt Rotkäppchen eine Jakobinermütze?: Über mutmaßliche Konotate bei Tieck und Grimm." In Joachim Bark, ed. *Literatursoziologie.* Vol. 2: *Beiträge zur Praxis.* Stuttgart: Kohlhammer. 159-80. Translated as "Is Little Red Riding Hood Wearing a Liberty Cap?" In Dundes, ed. 1989, 89-120.

1974. Richter, Dieter, and Johannes Merkel. *Märchen, Phantasie und Soziales Lernen.* Basis Theorie, 4. Berlin: Basis Verlag.

1974a. Rölleke, Heinz. "'Die Marburger Märchenfrau': Zur Herkunft der KHM 21 und 57." *Fabula* 15: 87-94. Reprinted in Rölleke. 1985, 55-63.

1974b. Rölleke, Heinz. "Die Urfassung der Grimmschen Märchensammlung von 1810: Eine Rekonstruktion ihres tatsächlichen Bestandes." *Euphorion* 68: 331-36. Reprinted in Rölleke. 1985, 26-32.

1974. Wetzel, Hermann Hubert. *Märchen in den französischen Novellensammlungen der Renaissance.* Berlin: Erich Schmidt.

1975. Barchilon, Jacques. *Le Conte merveilleux français de 1690 à 1790: Cent ans de féerie et de poésie ignorées de l'histoire littéraire.* Bibliothèque de la Revue de la littérature comparée, 114. Paris: Champion.

1975. Bucknall, Barbara J. "'La belle au bois dormant' par Perrault." *The Humanities Association Review / La Revue de l'Association des Humanités* (formerly *Humanities Association Bulletin*) 26: 96-105.

1975. Huss, Roy. "Grimms' 'The Table, the Ass and the Stick': A Drama of the Phallic Stage." *Psychoanalytic Review* 62: 165-71.

1975. Laruccia, Victor. "Little Red Riding Hood's Metacommentary: Paradoxical Injunction: Semiotics and Behavior." *Modern Language Notes* 90: 517-34.

1975a. Lüthi, Max. *Das Volksmärchen als Dichtung: Äestheik und Anthropologie.* Studien zur Volkserzählung, 1. Düsseldorf and Cologne: Diederichs. Translated by Jon Erickson as *The Fairytale as Art Form and Portrait of Man.* Bloomington: Indiana University Press, 1984.

1975b. Lüthi, Max. "Von der Freiheit der Erzähler: Anmerkungen zu einigen Versionen des 'Treuen Johannes.'" In W. van Nespen, ed. *Miscellanea Prof. Em. Dr. K. C. Peters: Door Vrienden en Collega's hem aangeboden ter gelegenheid van zijn emeritaat.* Antwerp: Govaerts. 458-72.

1975. Minard, Rosemary, ed. *Womenfolk and Fairy Tales.* Boston: Houghton Mifflin.

1975- . Ranke, Kurt, et al, eds. *Enzyklopädie des Märchens: Handwörterbuch zur historischen und vergleichenden Erzählforschung.* Berlin and New York: de Gruyter. Planned for 12 volumes.

1975. Rölleke, Heinz. "Die 'stockhessischen' Märchen der 'alten Marie': Das Ende eines Mythos um die frühesten KHM-Aufzeichnungen der Brüder Grimm." *Germanisch-Romanische Monatsschrift* n.s. 25: 74-86. Reprinted in Rölleke. 1985, 39-54.

1975. Stone, Kay [F.]. "Things Walt Disney Never Told Us." In Claire R. Farrer, ed. *Women and Folklore.* Austin: University of Texas Press. 42-50. (*Women and Folklore* was first published in the *Journal of American Folklore*, no. 347 [Jan.-March 1975].)

1976. Bettelheim, Bruno. *The Uses of Enchantment: The Meaning and Importance of Fairy Tales.* New York: Knopf. Paperback ed. New York: Vintage Books, 1977.

1976. Birkhäuser-Oeri, Sibylle von. *Die Mutter im Märchen: Deutung der Problematik des Mütterlichen und des Mutterkomplexes am Beispiel bekannter Märchen.* Ed. Marie-Louise von Franz. psychologisch gesehen, 28-29. 7th ed. Stuttgart: Bonz, 1983.

1976. Courtès, Joseph. "Une lecture sémiotique de 'Cendrillon.'" In Joseph Courtès, ed. *Introduction à la sémiotique narrative et discursive: méthodologie et application.* Paris: Hachette. 109-38.

1976. Franz, Marie-Louise von. *Individuation in Fairy Tales.* New York and Zurich: Spring Publications.

1976. Murray, Timothy C. "A Marvelous Guide to Anamorphosis: Cendrillon ou la Petite pantoufle de verre." *Modern Language Notes* 91: 1276-95.

1976/1977. Nitschke, August. *Soziale Ordnungen im Spiegel der Märchen.* Vol. 1: *Das frühe Europa.* Vol. 2: *Stabile Verhaltensweisen in unserer Zeit.* problemata, 53-54. Stuttgart — Bad Cannstadt: frommann-holzboog.

1976. Röhrich, Lutz. *Sage und Märchen: Erzählforschung heute.* Freiburg im Breisgau: Herder.

1977. Dan, Illana. "The Innocent Persecuted Heroine: An Attempt at a Model for the Surface Level of the Narrative Structure of the Female Fairy Tale." In Heda Jason and Dimitri Segal, eds. *Patterns in Oral Literature.* World Anthropology, 51. The Hague: Mouton. 13-30.

1977. Demoris, René. "Du littéraire au littéral dans 'Peau d'âne' de Perrault." *Revue des Sciences Humaines* 166: 261-79.

1977. Girardot. N. J. "Initiation and Meaning in the Tale of Snow White and the Seven Dwarfs." *Journal of American Folklore* 90: 274-300.

1977. Lüthi, Max. *Märchenanalysen: Arbeitstexte für den Unterricht.* Stuttgart: Reclam.

1977. Schödel, Siegfried, ed. *Märchenanalysen.* Reclams Universal-Bibliothek, 9532. Stuttgart: Reclam.

1977. Storck, Edzard. *Alte und neue Schöpfung in den Märchen der Brüder Grimm.* Bietigheim in Württemberg: Turm Verlag.

1977. Tismar, Jens. *Kunstmärchen.* Sammlung Metzler, 177. Stuttgart: Metzler.

1978. Bauman, Richard. *Verbal Art as Performance.* Reprint. With supplementary essays by Barbara A. Babcock, Gary H. Gossen, Roger D. Abrahams, and Joel F. Sherzer. Prospect Heights. IL: Waveland Press, 1984.

1978. Hanks, Carole and D. T. Hanks, Jr. "Perrault's 'Little Red Riding Hood': Victim of the Revisers." *Children's Literature* 7: 68-77.

1978. Mourey, Liliane. *Introduction aux contes de Grimm et de Perrault: Histoire, structure, mise en texte.* Archives des Lettres Modernes: Études de Critique et d'Histoire Littéraire, 180. Paris: Lettres Modernes-Minard.

1978. Phelps, Ethel Johnston, ed. *Tatterhood and Other Tales: Stories of Magic and Adventure.* Old Westbury, NY: The Feminist Press.

1978a. Rölleke, Heinz. *Der wahre Butt: Die wundersamen Wandlungen des Märchens vom Fischer und seiner Frau.* Cologne and Düsseldorf: Diederichs.

1978b. Rölleke, Heinz. "Zur Vorgeschichte der Kinder- und Hausmärchen: Bislang unbekannte Materialien im Nachlaß der Brüder Grimm." *Euphorion* 72: 102-05. Reprinted in Rölleke. 1985, 33-38.

1978. Woods, William. "Sleeping Beauty and the Art of Reading Fairy Tales." *CEA Critic: An Official Journal of the College English Association* 40, no. 2: 18-22.

1979. Bange, Pierre. "Comment on devient homme: Analyse sémiotique d'un conte de Grimm 'Les douze frères.'" In Georges Brunet, ed. *Études allemandes: Recueil dédié à Jean-Jacques Anstett.* Lyon: Presses Universitaires de Lyon. 93-138.

1979. Dégh, Linda. "Grimms' *Household Tales* and Its Place in the Household: The Social Relevance of a Controversial Classic." *Western Folklore* 38: 83-103.

1979. Gilbert, Sandra M. and Susan Gubar. *The Madwoman in the Attic: The Woman Writer and the Nineteenth-Century Literary Imagination.* New Haven: Yale University Press, 1984.

1979. Mowshowitz, H. H. "'Voir est un acte dangereux': An Analysis of Perrault's 'La Barbe bleue.' *Proceedings of the Pacific Northwest Conference on Foreign Languages*. 3, nos. 1-2: 28-30.

1979. Röhrich, Lutz. "Der Froschkönig und seine Wandlungen." *Fabula* 20: 170-92.

1979. Rölleke, Heinz. "Märchen von einem, der auszog, das Fürchten zu lernen: Zu Überlieferung und Bedeutung des KHM 4." *Fabula* 20: 193-204. Reprinted in Rölleke. 1985, 147-60.

1979. Rowe, Karen E. "Feminism and Fairy Tales." *Women's Studies: An Interdisciplinary Journal* 6: 237-57.

1979. Zipes, Jack. *Breaking the Magic Spell: Radical Theories of Folk and Fairy Tales*. Austin: University of Texas Press; London: Heinemann.

1980. Bausinger, Hermann. "Anmerkungen zu Schneewittchen." In Brackert, ed. 1980. 39-70.

1980a. Brackert, Helmut, ed. *Und wenn sie nicht gestorben sind [...]: Perspektiven auf das Märchen*. edition suhrkamp, 973. Frankfurt am Main: Suhrkamp.

1980b. Brackert, Helmut. "Hänsel und Gretel oder Möglichkeiten und Grenzen literaturwissenschaftlicher Märchen-Interpretation." In Brackert, ed. 1980, 9-38; 223-39.

1980. Bottigheimer, Ruth B. "The Transformed Queen: A Search for the Origins of Negative Female Archetypes in Grimms' Fairy Tales." *Amsterdamer Beiträge zur neueren Germanistik* 10: 1-12.

1980. Capellen, Renate Meyer zur. "Das schöne Mädchen: Psychoanalytische Betrachtungen zur 'Formwerdung der Seele' des Mädchens." In Brackert, ed. 1980, 89-119.

1980. Fetscher, Iring. "Von einem tapferen Schneider: Versuch einer soziologisch-sozialhistorischen Deutung." In Brackert, ed. 1980, 120-36.

1980. Göttner-Abendroth, Heide. *Die Göttin und ihr Heros: Die matriarchalen Religionen in Mythos, Märchen und Dichtung*. 3rd ed. Munich: Frauenoffensive, 1983.

1980. Lüderssen, Hans. "Hans im Glück: Kriminal-psychologische Betrachtungen — mit einem Seitenblick auf die Genese sozialer Normen." In Brackert, ed. 1980, 137-52.

1980. Nitschke, August. "Aschenputtel aus der Sicht der historischen Verhaltensforschung." In Brackert, ed. 1980, 71-88.

1980. Stolleis, Michael. "Der Ranzen, das Hütlein und das Hörnlein." In Brackert, ed. 1980, 153-64.

1981. Phelps, Ethel Johnston, ed. *The Maid of the North: Feminist Folk Tales from Around the World*. New York: Holt, Rinehart and Winston.

1981. Ritz, Hans. *Die Geschichte vom Rotkäppchen: Ursprünge, Analysen, Parodien eines Märchens*. 10th rev. and exp. ed. Göttingen: Muri, 1992.

1981. Zago, Ester. "Giambattista Basile: Il suo pubblico et il suo metodo." *Selecta: Journal of the Pacific Council on Foreign Languages* (formerly *Proceedings of the Northwest Conference on Foreign Languages*) 2: 78-80.

1982. Bottigheimer, Ruth B. "Tale Spinners: Submerged Voices in Grimms' Fairy Tales." *New German Critique* 27:141-50.

1982. Dundes, Alan, ed. *Cinderella: A Folklore Casebook.* Garland Folklore Casebooks, 3. New York and London: Garland.

1982. Scherf, Walter. *Lexikon der Zaubermärchen.* Kröners Taschenausgabe, 472. Stuttgart: Kröner.

1982. Waelti-Walters, Jennifer. *Fairy Tales and the Female Imagination.* Montreal: Eden Press.

1983. Ellis, John M. *One Fairy Story too Many: The Brothers Grimm and Their Tales.* Chicago: University of Chicago Press.

1983. Jones, Steven Swann. "The Structure of Snow White." *Fabula* 24,1-2: 56-71. Reprinted in Bottigheimer, ed. 1986, 165-86.

1983. McDowell, Edwin. "A Fairy Tale by Grimm Comes to Light." *The New York Times* 28 September: 1, 21.

1983a. Rölleke, Heinz. "'Schneeweißchen und Rosenrot: Rätsel um ein Grimmsches Märchen." *Wirkendes Wort* 33: 152-63. Reprinted in Rölleke. 1985, 191-206.

1983b. Rölleke, Heinz. "August Stöbers Einfluß auf die *Kinder- und Hausmärchen* der Brüder Grimm: Zur Textgenese der KHM 5 und 15." *Fabula* 24: 11-20. Reprinted in Rölleke. 1985, 75-87.

1983. Schenda, Rudolf. "Märchen erzählen —Märchen verbreiten: Wandel in den Mitteilungsformen einer populären Gattung." In Klaus Doderer, ed. *Über Märchen für Kinder von heute: Essays zu ihrem Wandel und ihrer Funktion.* Weinheim and Basel: Beltz. 25-43. Translated as "Telling Tales—Spreading Tales: Change in the Communicative Forms of a Popular Genre." In Bottingheimer, ed. 1986, 75-94.

1983a. Zipes, Jack. *Fairy Tales and the Art of Subversion: The Classical Genre for Children and the Process of Civilization.* New York: Wildman.

1983b. Zipes, Jack. *The Trials and Tribulations of Little Red Riding Hood: Versions of the Tale in a Sociocultural Context.* South Hadley, MA: Bergin and Garvey.

1984. Darnton, Robert. *The Great Cat Massacre and Other Episodes in French Cultural History.* New York: Basic Books.

1984. Jason, Heda. "The Fairy Tale of the Active Heroine: An Outline for Discussion." In Geneviève Calame-Griaule, Veronika Görög-Karady, and Michèle Chiche, eds. *Le conte, pourquoi? comment? / Folktales, why and how?* Actes des journées d'études en littérature orale: Analyse des contes - Problèmes et méthodes, Paris, 23-26 mars 1982. Paris: Centre national de la recherche scientifique. 79-97.

1984. Röhrich, Lutz. "The Quest of Meaning in Folk Narrative Research: What Does Meaning Mean and What Is the Meaning of Mean?" In McGlathery, ed. 1988, 1-15. Originally in *Scandinavian Yearbook of Folklore* 40: 125-38. Expanded version in German as "Zur Deutung und Bedeutung von Folklore-Texten." *Fabula* 26 (1985) : 3-28.

1985. Ellis, John M. "What Really Is the Value of the 'New' Grimm Discovery?" *The German Quarterly* 58: 87-90.

1985. Rölleke, Heinz. *"Wo das Wünschen noch geholfen hat": Gesammelte Aufsätze zu den Kinder- und Hausmärchen der Brüder Grimm.* Wuppertaler Schriftenreihe zur Literatur, 23. Bonn: Bouvier.

1985. Spörk, Ingrid. *Studien zu ausgewählten Märchen der Brüder Grimm: Frauenproblematik-Struktur-Rollentheorie-Psychoanalyse-Überlieferung-Rezeption.* Hochschulschriften Literaturwissenschaft, 66. Königstein im Taunus: Hain. 2nd ed. 1986.

1985. Stone, Kay F. "The Misuses of Enchantment: Controversies on the Significance of Fairy Tales." In Rosan A. Jordan and Susan J. Kalcik, eds. *Women's Folklore, Women's Culture.* Publications of the American Folklore Society, 8. Philadelphia: University of Pennsylvania Press. 125-45.

1986. Bauman, Richard. *Story, Performance, and Event: Contextual Studies of Oral Narrative.* Cambridge Studies in Oral and Literate Culture, 10. Cambridge: Cambridge University Press.

1986. Bottigheimer, Ruth B., ed. *Fairy Tales and Society: Illusion, Allusion and Paradigm.* Philadelphia: University of Pennsylvania Press.

1986. Dollerup, Cay, and Iven Reventlow. " A Case Study of Editorial Filters in Folktale: A Discussion of the 'Allerleirauh' Tales in Grimm." *Fabula* 27: 12-30.

1986. Dundes, Alan. "Fairy Tales from a Folkloristic Perspective." In Bottigheimer, ed. 1986, 259-69.

1986. Jason, Heda. "Genre in Folk Literature: Reflections on Some Questions and Problems." *Fabula* 27: 167-87.

1986. Jungblut, Gertrud. "Märchen der Brüder Grimm — feministisch gelesen." *Diskussion Deutsch: Zeitschrift für Deutschlehrer aller Schulformen in Ausbildung und Praxis* 91: 497-510.

1986. Oberfeld, Charlotte, and Wilhelm Solms, eds. *Das selbstverständliche Wunder: Beiträge germanistischer Forschung.* Marburger Studien zur Literatur, 1. Marburg: Hitzeroth.

1986. Rak, Michele. "Un nuovo modello di genere tra la societá letteraria barocca e le tradizioni della cultura popolare." In Giambattista Basile. *Lo Cunto de li cunti over Lo Trattenemiento de peccerile / Il Racconto dei racconti ovvero Il Passatempo per i più piccoli.* Michele Rak, ed. and trans. Milan: Garzanti.

1986. Richter, Dieter. "Wie Kinder Schlachtens mit einander gespielt haben (AaTh 2401): Von Schonung und Verschonung der Kinder — *in* und *vor* einem Märchen der Brüder Grimm." *Fabula* 27: 1-11.

1986a. Röhrich, Lutz. "Erotik im Volksmärchen: Ein Kulturhistorischer Exkurs." *Neue Zürcher Zeitung*. 1-2 February, no. 26: 91-92.

1986b. Röhrich, Lutz. "Das Bild der Frau im Märchen und im Volkslied." In Oberfeld and Solms, eds. 1986, 83-108.

1986c. Röhrich, Lutz. "'Der Froschkönig': Das erste Märchen der Grimm-Sammlung und seine Interpretation." In Oberfeld and Solms, eds. 1986, 7-41.

1986a. Rölleke, Heinz. "New Results of Research on *Grimms' Fairy Tales*." In McGlathery, ed. 1988, 101-11. Originally as "Neue Forschungsergebnisse zu den Grimmschen Märchen." In *Jacob und Wilhelm Grimm: Vorträge und Ansprachen*. Göttingen: Vandenhoeck & Ruprecht. 39-48.

1986b. Rölleke, Heinz. "Schneeweißchen und Rosenroth: KHM 161 in der Grimmschen Urfassung. Zwei bislang ungedruckte Briefe Wilhelm Hauffs an Grimm und ein Nachtrag zum *Fest der Unterirdischen*, einem frühen Zeugnis norwegischer Volksliteratur." *Fabula* 27: 265-87.

1986. Zipes, Jack, ed. *Don't Bet on the Prince: Contemporary Feminist Fairy Tales in North America and England*. New York: Methuen.

1987. Bottigheimer, Ruth B. *Grimms' Bad Girls and Bold Boys: The Moral and Social Vision of the Tales*. New Haven: Yale University Press.

1987. Tatar, Maria. M. *The Hard Facts of the Grimms' Tales*. Princeton: Princeton University Press.

1988. Bottigheimer. Ruth B. "From Gold to Guilt: Forces Which Reshaped Grimms' Tales." In McGlathery, ed. 1988, 192-204.

1988. Dégh, Linda. "What Did the Grimm Brothers Give to and Take from the Folk?" In McGlathery, ed. 1988, 66-89.

1988. Dundes, Alan. "Interpreting Little Red Riding Hood Psychoanalytically." In McGlathery, ed. 1988, 16-51. Reprinted in Dundes, ed. 1989, 192-236.

1988. Fink, Gonthier-Louis. "The Fairy Tales of the Grimms' Sergeant of Dragoons J. F. Krause as Reflecting the Needs and Wishes of the Common People." In McGlathery, ed. 1988, 146-63.

1988. Grätz, Manfred. *Das Märchen in der deutschen Aufklärung: Vom Feenmärchen zum Volksmärchen*. Stuttgart: Metzler.

1988. Hearne, Betsy. "Booking the Brothers Grimm: Art, Adaptations, and Economics." In McGlathery, ed. 1988, 220-33.

1988. McGlathery, James M., ed. *The Brothers Grimm and Folktale*. Urbana and Chicago: University of Illinois Press.

1988. Mieder, Wolfgang. "'Ever Eager to Incorporate Folk Proverbs': Wilhelm Grimm's Proverbial Additions in the Fairy Tales." In McGlathery, ed. 1988, 112-32.

1988. Nitschke, August. "The Importance of Fairy Tales in German Families before the Grimms." In McGlathery, ed. 1988, 164-77.

1988. Rölleke, Heinz, ed. *"Redensarten des Volks, auf die ich immer horche":* *Das Sprichwort in den Kinder- und Hausmärchen der Brüder Grimm.* With Lothar Bluhm. Sprichwortforschung, 11. Berne, etc.: Lang.

1988. Scherf, Walter. "Jacob and Wilhelm Grimm: A Few Small Corrections to a Commonly Held Image." In McGlathery, ed. 1988, 178-91.

1988. Stone, Kay F. "Three Transformations of Snow White." In McGlathery, ed. 1988, 52-65.

1988. Tatar, Maria M. "Beauties vs. Beasts in the Grimms' Nursery and Household Tales." In McGlathery, ed. 1988, 133-45.

1988. Ward, Donald. "New Misconceptions about Old Folktales." In McGlathery, ed. 1988, 91-100.

1988a. Zipes, Jack. *The Brothers Grimm: From Enchanted Forests to the Modern World.* New York and London: Routledge.

1988b. Zipes, Jack. "Dreams of a Better Bourgeois Life: The Psychosocial Origins of the Grimms' Tales." In McGlathery, ed. 1988, 205-19.

1989. Dégh, Linda. "Beauty, Wealth and Power: Career Choices for Women in Folktales, Fairy Tales and Modern Media." *Fabula* 30: 42-62.

1989. Dundes, Alan, ed. *Little Red Riding Hood: A Casebook.* Madison: University of Wisconsin Press.

1989. Zan, Yigal. "The Scientific Motivation for the Structural Analysis of Folktales." *Fabula* 30: 205-29.

1990. Broggini, Barbara. *"Lo cunto de li cunti" von Giambattista Basile: Ein Ständepoet im Streit mit der Plebs, Fortuna und der höfischen Korruption.* Europäische Hochschulschriften, ser. 9, no. 17. Bern, etc.: Lang.

1990. Warner, Marina. "Mother Goose Tales: Female Fiction or Female Fact?" *Folklore* (London) 101: 3-25.

1991. McGlathery, James M. *Fairy Tale Romance: The Grimms, Basile, and Perrault.* Urbana and Chicago: University of Illinois Press.

1992. Ziolkowski, Jan. "A Tale from before Fairy Tales: Egbert of Liège's 'De puella a lupellis seruata' and the Medieval Background of 'Little Red Riding Hood.'" *Speculum: A Journal of Medieval Studies* 67: 549-75.

INDEX